Towards a Geopolitical Image of Thought

Towards a Geopolitical Image of Thought

Gregg Lambert

EDINBURGH
University Press

Edinburgh University Press is one of the leading university presses in the UK. We publish academic books and journals in our selected subject areas across the humanities and social sciences, combining cutting-edge scholarship with high editorial and production values to produce academic works of lasting importance. For more information visit our website: edinburghuniversitypress.com

Edinburgh University Press Ltd
The Tun – Holyrood Road
12(2f) Jackson's Entry
Edinburgh EH8 8PJ

Typeset in 10.5/13pt Monotype Baskerville by
Servis Filmsetting Ltd, Stockport, Cheshire

A CIP record for this book is available from the British Library

ISBN 978 1 4744 8293 6 (hardback)
ISBN 978 1 4744 8296 7 (webready PDF)
ISBN 978 1 4744 8294 3 (paperback)
ISBN 978 1 4744 8295 0 (epub)

Contents

Acknowledgements

Earlier versions of some chapters have previously appeared in the following editions:

'Who are Deleuze and Guattari's Conceptual Personae?', in *Refrains of Freedom*, ed. Dorothea Olkowski and Constanine Boundas, Bloomington: Indiana University Press (2019).

'Two Meditations on "Becoming-Animal", Territory and the Origin of the Artwork', in *Deleuze and the Humanities: East and West*, ed. Rosi Braidotti, Kin Yuen Wong and Amy K. S. Chan, Continental Philosophy in Austral-Asia, Lanham: Rowman & Littlefield, 2018.

'Two Meditations on Becoming-Animal and the Work of Art', in *Deleuze and the Animal*, ed. Patricia MacCormack, Edinburgh: Edinburgh University Press, 2017.

'The "Non-Human Sex" in Sexuality: "What are Your Special Desiring Machines?"', in *Deleuze and Sex*, ed. Frida Beckman, Edinburgh: Edinburgh University Press, 2011, pp. 135–52.

'What the Earth Thinks', in *Deleuze and Space*, ed. Ian Buchanan and Gregg Lambert, Edinburgh: University of Edinburgh Press, 2005, pp. 220–39.

Abbreviations

A   Gilles Deleuze, *Deleuze A to Z (DVD)*, trans. Charles Stivalle, New York: Semiotext(e), 2011.

AO   Gilles Deleuze and Félix Guattari, *Anti-Oedipus: Capitalism and Schizophrenia*, vol. 1, trans. Robert Hurley, Mark Seem and Helen R. Lane, Minneapolis: University of Minnesota Press, 1983.

AOP   Guattari, *The Anti-Oedipus Papers*, New York: Semiotext(e), 2006.

ATP   Gilles Deleuze and Félix Guattari, *A Thousand Plateaus: Capitalism and Schizophrenia*, vol. 2, trans. Brian Massumi, Minneapolis: University of Minnesota Press, 1987.

BN   Jean-Paul Sartre, *Being and Nothingness*, trans. Hazel E. Barnes, New York: Washington Square Press, 1984.

CC   Gilles Deleuze, *Essays Critical and Clinical*, trans. Daniel W. Smith and Michael A. Greco, Minneapolis: University of Minnesota Press, 1997.

D   Jean-François Lyotard, *The Differend: Phrases in Dispute*, trans. Georges Van Den Abbeele, Minneapolis: University of Minnesota Press, 1988.

DI   Gilles Deleuze, *Desert Islands and Other Texts: 1953–1974*, trans. Michael Taormina, New York: Semiotext(e)/MIT Press, 2004.

DR   Gilles Deleuze, *Difference and Repetition*, trans. Paul Patton, London: The Athlone Press, 1994.

E   Jean-François Lyotard, *Enthusiasm: The Kantian Critique of History*, trans. Georges Van Den Abbeele, Palo Alto: Stanford University Press, 2009.

I   Jean-François Lyotard, *The Inhuman: Reflections on Time*, trans. Geoffrey Bennington and Rachel Bowlby, Palo Alto: Stanford University Press, 1992.

LS   Gilles Deleuze, *The Logic of Sense*, trans. Mark Lester and Charles Stivalle, New York: Columbia University Press, 1990.

N   Gilles Deleuze, *Negotiations*, trans. Martin Joughin, New York:
        Columbia University Press, 1995.
NP   Gilles Deleuze, *Nietzsche and Philosophy*, trans. Hugh Tomlinson,
        New York: Columbia University Press, 1983.
P   Gilles Deleuze, *Proust and Signs*, trans. Richard Howard, London:
        The Athlone Press, 2000.
PP   Immanuel Kant, *Perpetual Peace and Other Essays*, trans. Ted
        Humphry, Indianapolis: Hackett Publishers, 1983.
WP   Gilles Deleuze and Félix Guattari, *What is Philosophy?* trans.
        Hugh Tomlinson and Graham Burchell, New York: Columbia
        University Press, 1994.
Z   Friedrich Nietzsche, *Thus Spoke Zarathustra: A Book for All and None*,
        trans. Adrian del Caro, Cambridge: Cambridge University
        Press, 2006.

Preamble

This collection has been derived from essays and lectures written over the period of the last twenty years and is not intended as an academic monograph with a unified theme that appeals to the most recent hot topic in contemporary philosophy, much less to the subfield of 'Deleuze Studies'. In fact, the title was merely a compromise formation with marketing in order to 'appear contemporaneous,' 'to belong to the current field', 'to fit in'. I have always suspected that books of philosophy (or 'quasi-philosophy') on the most recent trend or 'hot topic' appear as if they could be written by almost anyone, by no one in particular, as if there is a trans-individual and strictly impersonal subject of enunciation lurking behind every author who says 'I'. At the same time, with this statement I am not claiming that this book could have been written by no one else, or that 'I am an original'. I admit: 'I' am absolutely not 'an original'! (I hope the reader will not be too disappointed.) Rather, 'I' am only what is called in conventional terms 'a secondary reader', a 'critic' or 'a commentator'. If anyone has ever cared to read them, my previous writings have often addressed what I called 'the art of commentary' and the conceptual persona of the modern commentator, especially the so-called writer of secondary works on a particular philosopher. They would also recall more than a little humour and irony directed at those who Deleuze himself calls 'scholars and familiars', those who he said would only bring the author shame and sadness.[1] I have always taken this statement to heart and have tried to imagine that everything I have written on 'Deleuze', in particular, would create a little feeling of joy, and if not joy, at least I have imagined it would make him smile.

In a short interview that appears in *Negotiations*, Deleuze himself affirms the role of what he calls 'mediators' (*'intercessors'*), and even says he needs his mediators to express himself, and his mediators cannot express themselves without him. It is this mutual dependency between a philosopher and his or her mediators that conditions the formation of a distinctive kind of collective identification that is particular to philosophy, but not unique, since it has its origins in early religions. In this regard, we need to remember that the philosophies of the Greeks were early religions, and in Part I I make reference to Lucian's *Lives for Sale*, in which the Roman poet satirises the early philosophies of Asia Minor as a nomadic band of celestial strangers and sages (including Christians and Jews) who wander around the continental peninsula selling snake oil and iconic images of 'the good life'. Second, we should also recall that the proper names of 'Mark', 'Matthew', 'Luke' and 'John' do not designate individual authors, but rather anonymous mediators of early Christian communities in Palestine, Jerusalem, Asia Minor and Constantinople. It is perhaps in this archaic manner that Deleuze refers to the formation of the link between mediators and minority communities in the work by Canadian filmmaker Pierre Perrault, which he calls 'legending', after Perrault, or what Bergson calls 'fabulation' (N: 125–6). Of course, Deleuze also extends this community to include plants and animals, as in the case of Castendada, and one could also include the community of Zarathustra and his animals as I will address in Part I on the role of conceptual personae in in the philosophy of Nietzsche. 'Whether they're real or imaginary,' Deleuze says, 'you have to form your mediators' (N: 125). For example, Nietzsche needed to invent his own mediators because he was the most solitary philosopher.

Mediators need the philosopher in order to speak, to say 'I', since they lack the power to speak for themselves, in their own name; however, philosophers also need their mediators or their conceptual persona in order to establish their own image of thought. It is obvious that Deleuze and Guattari served as mediators for each other's thoughts, which is to say, each understood 'in his own way' the thought put forward by the other, constituting what Deleuze calls 'a reflective series with two terms' in which each 'falsifies' the image of thought belonging to the other (N: 126). In other words, a Deleuze-thought 'falsifies' a Guattari thought and sends it back to him fundamentally or even imperceptibly changed; in turn, a Guattari-thought 'falsifies' a Deleuze-thought by providing a new intensity, a different syntax, or adding a new term, and so on and so forth. According to this merry-go-round, it is obvious that there can no longer be anything called 'an original thought', which is immediately forgotten after the first turn, but only a constant transformation that Deleuze compares to a 'baker's transformation': 'You take a square, pull it into a rectangle, cut the rectangle in half, stick it back on top of the other . . . after a certain number of transformations any two points, however close they may have been in the original square, are bound to end up in different halves' (N: 124).

What is the difference between this kind of transformation that occurs between the philosopher and his or her mediators, either real or imaginary, and the one that occurs between the philosopher and his or her commentators? As I have written previously, all commentaries lie when they represent the philosopher's image of thought and then claim it is true or an original image. However, lying must be first be understood in a non-moral sense as both Nietzsche and Deleuze understood it, since this is how they both understand the creation of truth. As Deleuze says, 'to say that "truth is created" implies that the production of truth involves a series of operations that amount to working on a material – strictly speaking, a series of falsifications' (N: 126). Thus, commentators don't necessarily lie when they represent the philosopher's thought as true or original – this can be excused as a rhetorical flourish or creative emphasis, a passion for the idea, or an intensive sign of either love or hatred for what the thought expresses in the body – and yet, all commentators do lie when they sign the truth with the philosopher's name rather than their own. It is here that we witness the birth of the conceptual persona of a particular philosopher or an entire philosophy (as when we commonly say 'Cartesianism', 'Kantianism', 'Hegelianism', and today when we say 'Deleuzian' or 'Derridean').

But here we must ask: why are commentators not able to sign with their own names? In other words, why do commentaries even exist? It is not because commentators cannot think, speak or write, but rather because they feel they do not have the power to create their own 'body without organs', as Deleuze first employs this term from Antonin Artaud's image of a purely an-organic and intensive image of thought. Therefore, on one level, we might posit an original shame the basis of the act of commentary, a feeling of lack, of having no body of their own that first motivates the commentator to combine with this other more powerful body of a philosopher in order to clothe their own naked body with a philosopher's words, that is, to have the power to say 'I'. Therefore, it is because not every subject is capable of either making or fabricating a body without organs from their own native powers that most commentaries exist like the secondary natures fashioned by little demiurges in gnostic myths.

This might reintroduce a psychological or moral dimension into our portrait of the conceptual persona, since the consciousness of the commentator must always be defined or diagnosed (as Deleuze would say, following Nietzsche) as a 'reactive consciousness'. However, his should not immediately be understood negatively, since all consciousness is in a certain sense reactive, but simply as the physical condition that occasions the form of commentary to even exist, like the existence of a wave in the ocean: every commentator first feels that they have no body without organs of their own, and thus must borrow another more powerful body as the cause of their saying 'I'. Otherwise, everyone would be capable of creating an original philosophy, which is to say that everyone would have the power to fabricate an image of pure an-organic life, of producing a body without organs, that is, an impersonal and collective image of a purely immanent life. However, in the original encounter between consciousness and the body without organs, consciousness reacts to the existence of another more powerful body with either acceptance and gratitude or resentment and even hatred towards this more powerful image of life, thereby producing in self-consciousness what Nietzsche called a 'spirit of revenge'.

One of Deleuze's earliest works, *Nietzsche and Philosophy*, creates a diagnosis of the psychology of resentment as one of the most dominant traits in the history of Western philosophy. Thus, in the history of all philosophical, literary and artistic commentary as well, one can immediately discern a spirit of resentment that disfigures and mutilates the original and more powerful body of the creator or the author, in order to separate this more powerful body from its own affects, its own expression, even to turn it against itself, to contradict its own statements as many philosophers have so often complained. Despite the fact that many of these commentaries are often dressed up as the philosopher's most intimate friends, or even 'disciples', just as what has occurred in the history of Christianity, it is a shame that these very same disciples have often betrayed the pure image of an-organic life by turning it into 'a school' or 'a church' – of course, there is an essential relationship between these two institutions in the history of philosophy as a result of the Christian history of the West! Perhaps this is one of the sources of what Deleuze refers to as the double shame of the 'Scholar and the Familiar', and, just as in the case of original sin, this first appears in the feeling of shame concerning one's own body, a feeling that must be negated, disguised and displaced onto the reader, or community of readers, and this is the problem that I will take up in Part I concerning the relation between the philosopher and his or her conceptual personae.

Much has been written in the history of philosophy on the subjects of apprenticeship and learning. Rather than cover the entire literature on the subject, I will simply quote an early passage from *Difference and Repetition* that has inspired my own understanding of the function of commentary:

> We learn nothing from those who say: 'Do as I do'. Our only teachers are those who tell us to 'do with me', and are able to emit signs to be developed in heterogeneity rather than propose gestures for us to reproduce. In other words, there is no ideo-motivity, only sensory-motivity. When a body combines some of its distinctive points with those of a wave, it espouses the principle of repetition which is no longer that of the Same, but involves the Other – involves difference, from one and one gesture to another, and carries that difference through repetitive space thereby constituted. (DR: 23)

Recalling the image of the wave that represents thought as the power of an-organic life, the above passage provides a precise image of the body of a commentary (or the 'text', if you like) as a 'space of distinctive points that combine with another body' (a wave, in this case, the primary body composed by Deleuze's thought). The difference between these two bodies is a third wave constituted in the space that is 'fabricated' by the commentator, producing both the displacement and disguise of the primary wave. Therefore, 'to learn is indeed to constitute this space through an encounter with signs, and repetition takes place and at the same time, disguising itself in the form of the commentary' (DR: 23).[2] Thus, commentary is an art because ultimately it is a creative act; even though the commentator does not create concepts, like the philosopher, he or she creates 'an encounter between signs', which according to the above analogy, resembles two waves breaking against each other with all the force of two obese sumo wrestlers, and then suddenly a third wave rises up white crowned and turbulent at its crest, like a frozen image that extinguishes all movement for an instant, before it topples over and crashes down. It is the frozen profile of the third wave that represents for me the image of thought as an instantaneous encounter that can only be measured in 'Planck time', and which only the best commentators have the necessary force to produce, that is, when they are done well.

Now that we have covered the preliminaries concerning who 'I' am and, thus, who 'I' am not – remember: 'I am not an original' and have never claimed being one! – at this point I will turn to the second part of this collection which also furnishes the title-theme on the 'geopolitical image of thought' (although, I have already admitted that this title was partly contrived for marketing purposes). Nevertheless, this image has preoccupied my works on Deleuze and Guattari from the very beginning and is mainly inspired by my reading of *A Thousand Plateaus* in the mid-1980s, and especially the inspiration of their last work, *What is Philosophy?* (1991), which I can truthfully say has been the focus of all my commentary over the past twenty years. If we recall the sections of the first part on 'Philosophy', they are: 1. The Concept; 2. The Plane of Immanence; 3. Conceptual Personae; 4. Geophilosophy. These can be understood as the four elemental components in response to the question: 'What is philosophy?' Given the proximity of the last two components, 'Conceptual Personae' and 'Geophilosophy', I have decided to follow the same order in my application of these same components to the minor question: 'What is "continental" philosophy?'

As Deleuze and Guattari wrote, 'the role of conceptual personae is to show thought's territories, its absolute deterritorializations and reterritorializations' (WP: 61).

> Whether physical, psychological, or social, deterritorialization is relative insofar as it concerns the historical relationship of the earth with the territories that take shape and pass away on it, its geological relationship with eras and catastrophes, its astronomical relationship with the cosmos and the stellar system of which it is a part. But deterritorialization is absolute when the earth passes into the pure plane of immanence of a Being-thought, of a Nature-thought of infinite diagrammatic movements. Thinking consists in stretching out a plane of immanence that absorbs the earth (or rather, 'adsorbs' it). (WP: 88)

Therefore, 'thinking [always] takes place in the relationship of territory and the earth' (WP: 85). To apply the last statement axiomatically, in Part I I seek to redraw the map of what has been called 'continental philosophy', mostly in the Anglo-American university as a result of the dominance of this institutional model globally, in which 'continental philosophy' is often defined in opposition to the national-linguistic tradition of 'analytic philosophy'.

In pursuing a new image of thought (i.e., a new formation of the relationship between a territory and the plane of immanence) by redefining this tradition of philosophy, no longer according to its national or institutional division, but rather according to a 'geopolitical image of thought', I return to a very early essay written by Deleuze in 1953 where he first presents the major conception of difference in two conflicting images of the Earth (the 'Absolute Ground' from which all philosophy arises) in the geological distinction between a 'continental' and an 'oceanic' island: 'Continental islands are "borne of fracture and disarticulation"', whereas 'Oceanic islands are originary and essential' (DI: 9).

In applying this geological division to the image of thought of contemporary philosophy over the past forty years so or so, I ask whether a concept of difference that is equally 'borne of fracture and disarticulation' can be understood *to ground* what I identify as three major philosophies of difference: the philosophies of Deleuze, Derrida and Lyotard. Taking up this question in Part I, I propose to redraw the former map of 'continental philosophy' simply by observing that the concept of difference these three philosophers have introduced has been accompanied by a movement of deterritorialisation from Europe to other territories globally, a movement that has recently veered towards an absolute deterritorialisation of the former ground of philosophy (i.e., Greece), or to quote from the passage above, at least towards 'a plane of immanence that absorbs the earth (or rather, "adsorbs" it)'. As a result, I argue, a new philosophy of difference in which 'geography and imagination are one' (DI: 9), as well as a new image of thought that 'takes place in the relationship of territory and the earth' (WP: 85), has today effectively deterritorialised the earlier meaning of 'continental philosophy', which can no longer be territorialised on the 'Oceanic island' of Europe.

At the same time, it is crucial to point out that this movement of deterritorialisation is not an abstraction, but characterises the concrete and physical movement of these three philosophers, in particular, whose conceptual personae can be found in multiple territories and languages. Of course, Derrida was by far the more frequent flyer and often travelled and taught in the United States, beginning in the 1950s, and Lyotard soon followed to the same house in Laguna Beach they both lived in during their separate teaching stints at the University of California, Irvine. Although Guattari travelled internationally to places like Brazil and Japan, Deleuze did not leave his apartment in Paris, but his conceptual persona certainly did and one cannot read a journal in Continental Philosophy today in any language without seeing an article on Deleuze's philosophy, nor could one attend an international conference without seeing his name in the proceedings. Once again, conceptual personae are not necessarily identical with the philosopher, so it does not really matter if Deleuze rarely left his arrondissement. In other words, just as occurred in the first century CE across the continental peninsula of Asia Minor and around the Mediterranean to the northern coast of Africa, which Deleuze and Guattari define as the original plane of immanence or 'milieu' of philosophy, today this former 'milieu' has become reterritorialised onto Asia and the Pacific Rim. For example, is it merely accidental that one of the few pictures we have of Deleuze outside his arrondissement in Paris or in the smoky seminar room of Paris VIII is sitting on the beach near Malibu, or that one of Lyotard's books is consecrated to 'Le Mur du Pacifique'?[3]

In turn, this movement has gone further, as a second generation, mostly from Australia and the United States, have travelled East and bring their conceptual personae to universities in Asia. Recalling the satire by Lucian, in which early philosophers are described as carpetbaggers, recently we can find nomadic bands of 'Deleuzians' selling their own plans of 'immanence' in India, China, Japan, Korea and elsewhere around the Pacific Rim. Conceptual personae have multiplied and populated new territories: an Australian 'Deleuze'; a Japanese 'Guattari'; a Chinese 'Derrida' or 'Althusser'; a Korean 'Deleuze' or 'Lacan'. In response to this frightening movement of deterritorialisation, European philosophers have attempted to reterritorialise philosophy again onto Europe and its past by recodifying their concepts on the original Greek, the Latin catechism or Roman law; or by instituting their plane of immanence on the universal language of mathematics, which has always functioned surreptitiously as an autochthonic language. There is even a new 'French Deleuze' and 'French Derrida' today as younger generations of French scholars claim that the prerequisite for understanding their philosophy is being native French, if not Parisian, and I have even heard this claim from Japanese and Korean elites who studied in Paris and learned to master the pronunciation of 'Deleuze' in a standard Parisian accent. (I confess I have always found this kind of linguistic snobbery distasteful, which underlies what Derrida has called 'philosophical nationalism', a spirit that has been prevalent especially and historically in the French, German and English academies.)[4] As I have been involved in this movement from early on, if not its very beginning, I have also found it somewhat telling that deterritorialisation does not move in the other direction, East to West, or East to West, depending from where one starts out on the map. Nevertheless, these concerted efforts to reterritorialise philosophy again on its 'originary and essential' Oceanic island will not work, given that the moment these philosophers believe they have landed once again on firm ground they are swept back out to sea and suddenly find themselves shipwrecked somewhere off the coasts of Brazil or Taiwan.

At this point, some readers might complain that the map I have redrawn is too fantastical and could be compared to one of those fabulous Chinese panels from the Qing Dynasty or a fable by Borges. On the contrary, I have portrayed this movement of deterritorialisation in the most concrete and literal of terms to show that something has fundamentally changed the image of thought that is expressed by contemporary philosophy today. In fact, the ground of reason itself has shifted and can no longer oriented by the history of European philosophy. In part, Deleuze and Guattari fail to understand this shifting ground when they continue to orient philosophy's plane of immanence to the territory of Greece, as well as the history of capitalism to the sovereignty of European reason. As they write, 'the infinite movement of thought, what Husserl calls *Telos*, must enter into conjunction with the great relative movement of capital that is continually deterritorialised in order to secure the power of Europe over all other peoples and their reterritorialisation on Europe' (WP: 98). At the same time, they also confess that 'Europeanization does not constitute a becoming but merely the history of capitalism, which prevents the becoming of subjected peoples' (WP: 98). Today it is clear that there is no longer any ideal of 'becoming-European' as the providential narrative of universal history, and are no existing 'peoples' (even those new peoples on the continent of Europe itself) who would ever subject themselves to such a 'destiny'. Moreover, they could not see from the own historical vantage point of the relative deterritorialisation of Europe by emerging global market capitalism, and their continued belief in the Marxian narrative of universal history, that capitalism today very well continue to occupy the absolute limit deterritorialisation, but its relative limit can no longer be reterritorialised on Europe, but instead on China and the United States. Thus, philosophy is no longer reterritorialised on Greece as a form of its own past, but rather on 'the outside' as a form of its own future. In my view, it is only Lyotard who foresaw this when he claimed that the principle of reason itself has become fractured by the differend, or by multiple differends, and what Kant called the regulative idea of the world has broken up into an archipelago of continental islands. Consequently, I conclude Part I by turning to Lyotard's major concept of difference as providing us with at least an 'sketch' (*Entwurf*) of what I am calling a new geopolitical image of thought. If we can acknowledge this new image of thought, it may be more accurate to call the contemporary tradition 'geopolitical philosophy' and no longer 'continental philosophy,' since today there is more than one continent and the original continent of Europe has become an archipelago of continental islands.

Part II, 'On the Pedagogy of Concepts', might be best represented as a philosophical miscellany or glossary. French academic philosophy has exhibited a penchant for this genre, and Deleuze himself argued that such a constructive exercise is needed since philosophers create new concepts, but they are not good at communicating the nature of the problems that the new concept is supposed to resolve (N: 136). Without understanding the pragmatic nature of the problem-solving approach in the construction of new concepts, concepts themselves are in danger of being misunderstood as essences, as eternal ideas, and even as 'miracles' (what Spinoza called 'confused ideas'). Of course, there are many concepts in the history of philosophy, but also in Deleuze's philosophy, that have been badly misunderstood or confused in this manner. Deleuze explains the construction of new concepts very simply:

> Creating concepts is constructing some area in the plane [of immanence], adding a new area to existing ones, exploring a new area, filling in what's missing . . . If new concepts have to be brought in all the time, it's just because the plane of immanence has to be constructed area by area, constructed locally, going from one point to the next. (N: 147)

Because a concept is never given in the first place, or when it is taken up, this is why Deleuze says there are no simple concepts, and every concept has several components, is a multiplicity, even so-called 'first concepts' (i.e., categories, a priori ideas, etc.). Moreover, as he claims, each concept has a *chiffre* (a combination, a key), and so to understand a particular concept one must know the combination to open it and examine its specific construction (WP: 15). In some way, the kind of pedagogy invoked could be compared to instructing how to break a lock or solve a puzzle, even though there is always an element of chance or luck in the creation of concepts, which is why Deleuze calls it an art rather than an exercise in logic. In Part II, I examine four concepts that belong to Deleuze (and Guattari's) philosophical glossary: 'another person' (*autrui*), 'desiring-machines', 'becoming-animal' and 'what is a territory?' I will not introduce them here, except to say that it is the concept of 'another person' (*autrui*) that has preoccupied me for over twenty years – and it is only recently that I come to believe that I have figured it out. As some will know its history, it first appears in *Proust and Signs* (1963) in relation to the mysterious visage of Albertine, and then again in the last chapter of *Difference and Repetition* (1969) where Deleuze adds more components primarily drawn from the philosophies of Leibniz and Sartre (a frightened face, a possible world, or the possibility of a frightening world). Finally, as I have written elsewhere, I find it significant that the concepts of 'another person' returns again in *What is Philosophy?* and is even offered as the first example of the pedagogy of the concept. As I wrote in *The Non-Philosophy of Gilles Deleuze* (2002):

> The creation of the concept of the Other Person represents perhaps the most profound and yet most subtle transformations in Deleuze's entire philosophical system, and it is not by accident that the concept of the Other Person is given as the first concept in *What is Philosophy?* – a place usually reserved for the concept of God as 'first principle' in traditional metaphysics (particularly the scholastic philosophy of Duns Scotus who bears a special importance for Deleuze).[5]

Perhaps today I would not make the same claim concerning the 'firstness' of the concept, except to say that, if the concept does not assume the place usually reserved for the concept of God in a traditional metaphysics, Deleuze's construction of the concept from the components he derives from other philosophies, and the manner in which he constantly returns to vary or add new components (i.e., to add a new area, to explore another, to fill in what is missing), is certainly the most exemplary of Deleuze's understanding of what he means when he says that, in a philosophy of expressionism, 'construction replaces reflection' in the communication of ideas (N: 147). In the last two concepts, 'becoming-animal' and 'a territory', I employ this sense of constructionism in asking how an artist can create 'a territory' in the work of art, and how 'a territory' in the artwork is related to the territories of animals. In examining this question through concept of 'becoming-animal' in the philosophy of Deleuze and Guattari, I discover the major role played by human sexuality, and I turn to the figure of Leonardo da Vinci and to Freud's famous biography of the artist to further demonstrate this claim. It is in the concept of 'territory' that I also return to a key component of a geopolitical image of thought.

To conclude, if I began the preface to this book by highlighting my understanding of my role as a commentator of Deleuze's philosophy over the last twenty years or so (who 'I' am, and thus, who 'I' am not), I will now end by saying this will be my last commentary. It is not because I no longer agree with Deleuze's philosophy, or because I've had enough, or even because I now believe I can 'go beyond' Deleuze (whatever that means). Rather, it is simply because I believe I have learned enough to feel that I am now capable of creating my own body without organs and thus, my long apprenticeship has been successfully concluded. Once again, as Deleuze said, 'we learn nothing from those who say: "Do as I do". Our only teachers are those who tell us to "do with me" and are able to emit signs to be developed in heterogeneity rather than propose gestures for us to reproduce' (DR: 23). Deleuze has been a good teacher in this respect, and his philosophy has emitted many signs that I have tried to develop in my own way to construct my conceptual persona, or my 'Deleuze'. In other words, or in the words of Chaucer, 'Go, little book . . .'. Whether it will find an attentive reader, or fall on deaf ears, is no longer 'my concern'. *It's out of my hands now.*

Notes

1. See Lambert, *The Non-Philosophy of Gilles Deleuze.* I wrote earlier: 'Most books of philosophy these days, particularly those written on other philosophers, which claim to explain, to clarify, and even in some cases to rectify the mistakes of the philosopher, all share in something deceitful and malicious. Indeed, they are often written from a certain spirit of "bad faith," although, certainly, not many commentators would admit that this is the source of their inspiration. On the contrary, many commentators spend their time before the reader's short-lived attention trying to persuade anybody who happens onto their little tome (in the library or bookstore, or even today on the internet) that it is absolutely worth the time it will take to read. They might argue that it will impart some new knowledge, or a new twist on something already known; perhaps it will serve other uses for the author' (p. ix).
2. Some passages from the above previously appeared in my homage to the commentary of Ronald Bogue. See Lambert, 'The Joy of Surfing with Deleuze and Guattari'.

3. Jean-François Lyotard, *Le Mur du Pacifique* (Paris: Galilée, 1979).
4. Derrida, *The Other Heading*, pp. 48–9.
5. Lambert, *The Non-Philosophy of Gilles Deleuze*, p. 10.

Who are Deleuze and Guattari's 'Conceptual Personae'?

1.

The above title should recall the small essay written by Heidegger in 1954, after the war, 'Who is Nietzsche's Zarathustra?'[1] This essay should remain in the background of my reflections on the philosopher and his or her 'conceptual personae'. Deleuze and Guattari introduce this unique figure in the third chapter of *What is Philosophy?*, arguing that every philosopher seeks to lay out a plan(e) of immanence in order to populate it with his or her own concepts, in contradistinction to notions belonging to religion and science, including those concepts it borrows from previous (and even 'antipathetic') philosophers (WP: 35–61). In order to accomplish this plan, first a conceptual persona must be invented to bring a philosophy to life, in short, to 'personalize philosophy', and, second, the plane of concepts must be connected to the image of thought following the coordinates that the conceptual persona lays out and according to the intensities that this image expresses. Otherwise, no one would be able to recognise who is speaking, or how this manner of speaking – this style of writing – is different from all the other philosophers who came before. As Deleuze and Guattari write, 'the conceptual persona is needed to create concepts on the plane, just as the plane needs to be laid out. But these two operations merge in the persona, which itself appears as a distinct operator' (WP: 64). In other words, if thinking is determined or often represented as and by an image that is distinctive from images of perception, memory, intuition or imagination, then the conceptual persona refers to a special agency of enunciation, which is not always identified with the subject of the individual philosopher.

By invoking this special agency (or faculty) that is found in philosophical enunciation alone, Deleuze and Guattari claim that philosophy constantly brings its distinctive conceptual personae to life; it gives life to them (WP: 62). But immediately we might ask, 'What kind of life?' 'How do conceptual personae actually live?' In replying to these questions, I will not return to the earliest of philosophy's conceptual personae (e.g., Plato's 'Socrates'), but rather to certainly the most 'lively' of all conceptual personae in the history of philosophy: Nietzsche's 'Zarathustra'. Thus, Heidegger's question and the accompanying article 'Who is Nietzsche's Zarathustra?' will serve as an important guide, after which I will return to Deleuze's own writings on the figure of Zarathustra from the earlier *Nietzsche and Philosophy* to create two very different portraits of Nietzsche's chief conceptual persona. First, the question 'who' is Nietzsche's Zarathustra must be given full value, which is to say, Zarathustra must be understood as *a unique individual* who stands apart from the philosopher himself. Accordingly, I will no longer place proper names in quotation marks.

First, to understand this form of individuation that belongs to a particular philosophy (or philosopher), the relation between a philosopher and the conceptual persona can determined by a notion of *Auseinandersetzung*, a self-feeling within the other. Deleuze and Guattari define this feeling as a special kind of empathy (*Einfühlung*), but which remains extremely ambiguous especially when they were writing together and following a movement of thinking that creates an empathic movement of two individuals attempting to think the same thought. In the case of the solitary figure of a philosopher such as Nietzsche, on the other hand, what does it means to say that a philosopher feels an empathy for his or her own thought in a manner that is not unrelated to a feeling of empathy for another person? For example, this feeling is something that Zarathustra will constantly express concerning the thought of the eternal return, even though he is not yet capable of thinking this great thought, that is to say, affirming all that it will demand concerning the overturning of current values, accompanied by a feeling that he is not yet deserving of his own thought. Nevertheless, Zarathustra's thought always remains close to him, like an intimate companion, expressing a form of intimacy that is yet unknown, and is figured in the image of a serpent that is coiled around the eagle's neck 'like a friend'. This empathetic image is the basis for the creation of a conceptual persona of Zarathustra as a relation between the thinker and his thought that also becomes the point where thought separates from the actual person of the philosopher, and allows thinking to become in ways that exceed the limits of the original thinker. As Deleuze and Guattari write:

The destiny of the philosopher is to become his conceptual persona or personae, at the same time that these personae themselves become something other than what they are historically, mythologically, or commonly (the Socrates of Plato, the Dionysus of Nietzsche, the Idiot of Nicholas of Cusa). The conceptual persona is the becoming or the subject of a philosophy, on a par with the philosopher, so that Nicholas of Cusa, or even Descartes, should have signed themselves 'the Idiot', just as Nietzsche signed himself 'the Antichrist' or 'Dionysus crucified'. (WP: 64)

Second, let us return once again to the question of why philosophers 'need' conceptual personae in the first place? In other words, why did Nietzsche *need* Zarathustra as his mouthpiece? Was it because he could not speak for himself, in his own name, that he needed partly to invent another persona who speaks for him (meaning *in his place*)? And yet, perhaps 'need' is not the right way to establish the relationship, and a better way of posing this question is to ask why Zarathustra was invented literally to serve as his 'loudspeaker'? The art of invention belongs to the history of rhetoric, as the invention of figures of speech, and poetics, as symbolic or poetic forms of invention. So, the invention of 'conceptual personae' addresses the specific rhetorical and poetic construction that belongs to philosophy as a discourse. And since philosophy deals with concepts, its personae are conceptual personae, rather than merely rhetorical figures, poetic symbols or heroic personae. In differentiating from the rhetorical figure of speech, or the poetic symbol, Deleuze and Guattari define something 'idiosyncratic' and, at the same time, 'impersonal' in the relation between the philosopher and his or her conceptual personae; hence, conceptual personae are not the representatives of the philosopher, but in fact actual subjects that have or are given the right to sign their own name, even though it often happens that the philosopher signs for them in the sense that Plato 'signed' for Socrates.

Third, being distinctive from a figure of speech, a rhetorical device or a discursive trope, conceptual personae are the very medium of philosophical enunciation, responding to our question above concerning why philosophers need conceptual personae in order to speak. It is the conceptual persona who says 'I', who thus institutes the relation between the expression of thought and the subject of the thinker, which is not the same identity as the individual who thinks, but instead refers to subjacent third person as the true subject of enunciation. Another example of this can also be found in Borges, who signs or writes of 'the other

Borges', in the third person, which no longer refers to the living Borges. As Deleuze recounts, there are numerous examples of this kind of enunciation in modern literature – such as Joyce's 'Bloom' or 'Stephen', Kafka's 'K.', Beckett's 'Molloy', 'Moran' or 'Mahood', Nevertheless, there is some characteristic that distinguishes the conceptual persona from all these literary personae, which I have already addressed previously in my writings on this subject.[2] This distinction has to do with the actuality of the conceptual personae that has a differential feature or composition apart from the typology of literary figures; although, as we know, Deleuze is often drawn to precisely those works where the difference between conceptual personae and literary figures blend and threaten to become indistinguishable, as if he is engaged in an incredible effort to tear away (even to steal) the potential of the concept from the aesthetic figure by installing the latter on a philosophical plane of immanence. For example, we can see this effort dramatically portrayed in his philosophical appropriation of the figure of 'Bartleby' from the late essay on Melville's fictional characters.

Nevertheless, recalling the question of 'how' conceptual persona are created or invented, there still remains a degree of mystery that continues to surround the technique of invention – apparently, even natural genius is not sufficient to give us any knowledge of this technique! – and it seems evident that Deleuze is always seeking to discover hints and clues in the figures invented by writers and artists that could lead to the invention of a unique conceptual persona that he could adapt to his own philosophical programme, or image of thought. The difference between the concept in philosophy and the percept and affect in art or literature is well known from the arguments put forward later in *What is Philosophy?* According to the often cited statement, philosophy lays out a plane of immanence and populates it with concepts, while art produces a composition of percepts and affects; 'thus, art thinks no less than philosophy, but it thinks through affects and percepts' (WP: 66). Although I have never been satisfied with this neat division of labour, or this Kantian description of the two specialised faculties of philosophy and art, according to which the plane of immanence and the knowledge of the concept belong to philosophy alone, while the planes of sensation and affection are ascribed to art, which can 'think' only through percepts and affects. After all, isn't this simply another version of the phallocentric division that already belongs to the history of philosophy?

Here, we need to highlight the dramatic situation of the tribunal that appears as the setting of *What is Philosophy?* The conceptual persona of the philosopher who appears there is not a neutral party to the question, according to the image of the Kantian legislator or judge. Instead, there are several subjects who appear, each of which seek to 'lay claim to the concept' (artists, writers, scientists, computer scientists, modern advertisers, etc.); however, it is only the philosopher who, according to Deleuze, lays claim to the concept 'by a species of right'. Hence, the conceptual persona of the modern philosopher that is created by Deleuze and Guattari is the subject who cries out before an indeterminate public in the age of mass communication: 'I lay claim to the concept', or 'I am the true friend of the concept'! The difference between this conceptual persona and the Kantian philosopher as legislator is profound, since today the philosopher is not already guaranteed the right to the concept and this creates the legal situation of needing the conceptual persona who will serve as a 'mediator' or as an 'advocate' (in the exemplary case of Nietzsche) to vigorously speak *on behalf of* the philosopher and his or her philosophy. As I will return to argue, it is in this manner that the situation posed by the title question of *What is Philosophy?* dramatically reactivates the original social situation of philosophy itself during the first century CE, when philosophers were nomadically dispersed across the territories of Asia Minor, and were engaged in battles, not only with other philosophers (Stoics, Cynics, Epicureans, Aristotelians and Platonists), but also with Gnostics, Christians, Jews and Eastern sages for the best conception of *a life*, or what Deleuze himself later names 'a life of pure immanence'.

Not surprisingly, it is Heidegger who most accurately intuits the relation between the creation of concepts and the importance of the conceptual persona in his small essay written in 1954, 'Who is Nietzsche's Zarathustra?' Turning to the essay itself, the first thing we should notice is that the question of 'who' is already the subject of Heidegger's interpretation, and we are immediately provided with an answer to this question, which is expressed by the first two words of the title of Nietzsche's work: '*Also sprach*'. Above all, Zarathustra is a 'speaker' who speaks in place of Nietzsche himself in this great epic poem; however, Heidegger interprets the discursive role of Zarathustra as an 'advocate' (*Fürsprecher*). Immediately, we can confirm two important characteristics that belong to Deleuze and Guattari's definition of the role of a conceptual persona:

1. The conceptual persona is the true subject of enunciation, the one who says 'I';
2. The philosopher needs the conceptual persona to objectify his or her own thinking, or image of thought.

Thus, Heidegger is the first to discern the function of Zarathustra as Nietzsche's own distinctive conceptual persona, as the creation of one who 'speaks for' or 'in place of' – but also, as we will discover later, 'before', as the one who precedes Nietzsche and who will even anticipate his complete philosophy! This role has also two distinct senses we must now track. The first sense of *fore* refers to both a temporal and a spatial location that will become important for understanding the nature of the enunciation we are dealing with here: Zarathustra speaks 'fore', meaning both 'before' Nietzsche and 'in advance of'. The second sense is that manner in which the figure of Zarathustra appears spatially 'before' Nietzsche (i.e., in front of Nietzsche). According to both senses, in order to grasp the function of the conceptual persona, we must see – but also hear – the discourse of Zarathustra from a temporal position that is *before* Nietzsche; however, this position also implies that Nietzsche (the philosopher himself) is either *after* or *behind*, that is to say, occupying a position of silence (or listening) since two subjects cannot be heard to speak at this same time without reducing the enunciation to babble.

This position is crucial if we are to understand the role of silence as a relation to Zarathustra's speech, and the multiple senses of silence that run throughout the poem (meditative, ruminative, dramatic, but also extremely comical). Moreover, it is only by locating the position of silence in each instance where either Zarathustra or one of the other characters can be heard to be speaking that we might also locate the true sense of Nietzsche's own expression. For example, at one point after Zarathustra returns home to his cave with his animals, Zarathustra himself falls into a profound silence, at which point his animals can be heard to say: 'Zarathustra, you are the teacher of the Eternal Return', a statement before which Zarathustra chooses to remain silent, and yet only pretends to be sleeping. It is only from the sense of this last silence that we might begin to discern Nietzsche's true enunciation. Consequently, when Zarathustra falls silent, we can hear the animals continuing to babble on, as if to distract him from his own deep thought. Zarathustra says to his animals: 'Just keep babbling and let me listen! It invigorates me so when you babble; where there is babbling indeed the world lies before me as a garden' (Z: 175).

In occupying a position of 'firstness', Zarathustra also speaks before Nietzsche in the sense of running out ahead and just blurting out whatever comes into his head, so that Nietzsche might be able to hear himself think and thereby have a relation to his own thought. This is related to the situation of solitude that is always underlined throughout the poem. It is a solitude in which the thought of Nietzsche (the philosopher), which is only hinted at by Zarathustra, still as of yet has neither language nor community, and thus Nietzsche is forced to invent an interlocuter for his dialogue with himself, in the same gesture that he names his animals as his only community. Nietzsche's solitude is so great that we often hear him ask himself ask through the spokesperson of Zarathustra: 'Do I myself even exist?' Because of this great solitude of the thinker alone with his own thought that we might begin to understand the need to create the conceptual persona of Zarathustra so that the philosopher Nietzsche is able to endure the extreme loneliness of his own thought. There is a minimal community established between the thinker and his own thought; Nietzsche listens to what Zarathustra says and remains silent. However, because it is Zarathustra who is doing all the speaking, Nietzsche himself should not be held completely responsible for everything that Zarathustra simply blurts out. In other words, there is a moral dimension of Nietzsche's own silence as well, and it is this moral dimension that has subsequently played out in all interpretations of Nietzsche's philosophy, including all the nefarious interpretations concerning what is said about the *Übermensch* in National Socialist commentaries, or those interpretations that mistakenly ascribe statements made by the conceptual persona of Zarathustra, or by one of his animals, to the philosopher himself (for example, the statement that 'you are the teacher of the Eternal Return', which I will return to below). This is partly why I have placed so much stress on that fact that, strictly speaking, Nietzsche says nothing in both a literal sense, but also legally and morally, 'on his own behalf'.

This moral aspect of the discursive situation leads us to a third sense contained in the image of the conceptual persona of Zarathustra as an 'advocate', in the sense that every philosophical enunciation must speak *for something, on behalf of something* or *in justification of something*. Simply put, all philosophical enunciation is *affirmative*, even when it is negative or destructive of established values. This can be understood as an axiom:

every philosophy affirms something, even when it denies, or affirms nothing is the place of something. ('Nothing' is still something, after all!) As Nietzsche himself argues in subsequent works like *Genealogy of Morals* and *The Gay Science*, even the most critical or negative philosophical enunciation remains an affirmation and thus *there is no philosophy that doesn't affirm something!* This is true even when the philosopher affirms 'unhappy consciousness' or the 'spirit of revenge', which are the representatives of the philosophy of the dialectic and the negative that appear as the greatest opponents in Zarathustra in the persona of the Last Man and of the Christian figure of the Ass who wears the skin of a lion, given that both philosophies affirm suffering and believe that the weight of their own suffering has value in itself. As the great synthesis of these two philosophies, the critical image of reason provided by post-Kantian philosophy only leads to what Heidegger called the closure of the history of metaphysics, which is to say, the overturning of this history into the full expression of Christian nihilism. This is because the role that critique and the negative play in removing all transcendental illusions as the basis of possible knowledge actually affirms *Nothing* in place of these illusions; however, critical philosophy remains powerless to actually transform values and thus can only appeal to a transcendent image of reason, or to scientific and secular reason after the death of God, in order to justify the destruction of all previous values.

As Deleuze writes concerning the impasse of Kantian critical philosophy from the perspective of a fully realised Nietzschean affirmative philosophy:

> In Kant, critique was not able to discover the truly active instance which would have been capable of carrying it through. It is exhausted by compromise: it never makes us overcome the reactive forces which are expressed in man, self-consciousness, reason, morality and religion. Rather, it even has the opposite effect – it turns these forces into something a little more 'our own'. (NP: 89)

Nietzsche's re-evaluation of this image of reason – which, moreover, is not expressed in the form of rejection, contradiction or critique – is illustrated in the beginning of the third part of *Zarathustra*, 'The Convalescent', which Heidegger focuses on almost exclusively, even though it is at this point he loses the path of Nietzsche's own thought by comparing 'convalescence' to the specific pathological symptoms of illness that he defines as 'homesickness'. It is around this point that we can see Heidegger importing his own conceptual persona into the interpretation of Nietzsche's philosophy, in the sense of dressing up Zarathustra according to his own persona. In fact, this might even explain the bizarre usage of the term 'pinafore' that appears in the etymological derivation of the meaning of 'fore', referring to a sleeveless dress worn over a skirt or dress by a young girl. (I have to confess, I started laughing the minute I had the image of Zarathustra dressed up as a little girl in a pinafore, which is to say, dressed up in a perverse manner I have often suspected of Heidegger himself.)

Rather than following Heidegger's interpretation of the third part of *Zarathustra*, 'The Convalescent', I will return to the original text in order to derive a sense of affirmation I have spoken about above. What do we find? First, against what we might expect of most convalescents, we might be surprised to be surprised to find Zarathustra not at home in bed, but scaling a great peak as a mountain climber! Perhaps he may very well be on the road to himself, which is the meaning that Heidegger gives to the figure of the mountain climber, but this road leads up before it suddenly turns downward into Zarathustra's infamous 'downgoing' (*Untergang*) which is where Heidegger both begins and ends his interpretation. On the other hand, if he began at the very commencement of the third part, and not back in the cave at the conclusion where Zarathustra is suddenly awaken up by his most abysmal thought and falls unconscious after being overcome by nausea, we might have a better understanding of the meaning of the abyss that Zarathustra is staring into – the abyss not only of Zarathustra himself but all of humanity!

Returning now to the beginning of the third part, 'The Wanderer', it is here that, as I have already stated, we find Zarathustra, the mountain climber: '"I am a wanderer and a mountain climber", he said to his heart. "I do not like the plains and it seems I cannot sit still for long."' It is this heady feeling, moreover, that will lead us to the first revelation of who Zarathustra is, which also occurs at the moment of his greatest danger, which is his sudden realisation that he could suddenly fall. In other words, the mountain must exist in order for Zarathustra to become a mountain climber and discover something about himself – 'that my own self and everything in it has been long abroad and scattered among all things and accidents' (Z: 121). Zarathustra stands before his 'last peak', the hardest part of his long hike, which is the abyss itself: 'Peak and abyss – they are now merged into one!' However, it is also at this point that another voice can be heard speaking, which is not the voice of one of the other characters since no one is there to listen, given that this moment is also described in the last line as the point of his 'loneliest hike'. Can we imagine that this voice is Zarathustra's interior thought speaking to him, or perhaps the silent voice of Nietzsche himself bidding Zarathustra to go farther to go onward and upward? The voice simply says: 'You go your way of greatness' (Z: 121). Immediately after this statement, we find the line: 'Thus Zarathustra spoke to himself as he climbed, comforting his heart with hard sayings . . .' Nevertheless, how are we to accept from this description of the narrator that the voice is Zarathustra's own? No, Zarathustra himself is silent, and his silence has become merged with Nietzsche's own silence. Perhaps it is the silence itself that can be heard speaking, which is the highest point of the mediation and external journey, the point where the mountain and the abyss have merged into one; or maybe it is the abyss itself, the voice of Zarathustra's own abyssal thought, which is also the ultimate summit of Nietzsche's thought of the 'Eternal Return'. In either case, this point marks the moment of 'turning' in the story, the beginning of Zarathustra's so-called 'downgoing' (i.e., the period of his convalescence), as he himself affirms in the following statement: '"I recognize my lot [my destiny]", he said at last, with sorrow. "Well then! I am ready. Just now my ultimate solitude began"' (Z: 121).

This feeling is familiar to all mountain climbers. It is evident from the penultimate description that at precisely the moment when Zarathustra (the mountain climber) reaches what he thought was his 'last peak', he suddenly discovers yet another summit that is enunciated by the abyss opened in his own thought; it says, 'you must climb over yourself – up, upward, until you have even your stars beneath you!' In this manner, the abyss now speaks from the summit of Nietzsche's most intimate thought, 'look down on myself and even on my stars; only that would I call my peak, that remains to me as my ultimate peak! – ' (Z: 121). In other words, it is here that we find the most crucial description of the figure of the 'Overman' in Nietzsche's philosophy, who is simply defined as someone able to climb on top of his own head ('how else would one climb upward?'), but also as the figure who is both above and below the conceptual persona of Zarathustra. However, at this point we also find that the conceptual persona of Zarathustra is no longer up in front, having been replaced by the figure of the Overman. Does this mean that Nietzsche can finally be heard to speak for himself, thus no longer having a need for an 'advocate', having now learned to recognise his own most intimate and abysmal thought (e.g. 'my peak', 'my ultimate peak')? In either case, since peak and abyss have already merged and are now one, we see the image of a new conceptual persona, the Overman, who is described as standing on a peak and looking downwards at the stars.

From this great height, which Nietzsche already describes as 'my peak', the Overman looks downwards at the stars, representing what is essentially a parody of the highest point imagined by Kantian transcendental philosophy. Thus, the Kantian perspective is drawn from *The Critique of Practical Reason* (and appears also on Kant's tombstone) and runs as follows: 'Two things fill the mind with ever-increasing wonder and awe, the more often and the more intensely the mind of thought is drawn to them: the starry heavens above me and the moral law within me.'[3] I have described Nietzsche's allusion to this statement as a parody of the transcendental origin of morality imagined by Kant (who appears elsewhere as 'The Last Man' or as 'The Legislator'), since, according to Nietzsche's representation, the stars themselves are 'beneath' the Overman and there is no accompanying reference to the moral law within. In fact, it is this revelation that creates a fundamental disorientation in the thinking of the highest values heretofore posed by philosophy, a disorientation that no longer knows in what direction to look for the source of the highest values, nor whether 'the moral law' can be actually be found to reside within the subject of Man, and this calls for the creation of a new conceptual persona of the so-called 'critical philosopher', as one who will actually be capable of trekking down the source of these former values (which Nietzsche accomplishes in *The Genealogy of Morals*) and then of founding the idea moral law on a new conception of Right (which is the plan for the unfinished *Will to Power*). In short, it calls for the creation of the conceptual persona of the philosopher as Overman.

At the same time, we should call attention to the fact that the conceptual persona of the Overman never makes an appearance in Zarathustra, qua persona or character, nor anywhere else in Nietzsche's philosophical oeuvre, except perhaps as the silent voice of the abyss. In fact, the figure of the Overman is invented by Nietzsche precisely as the future conceptual persona who stands above the figure of Zarathustra himself, meaning of a higher rank and order in Nietzsche's systematic philosophy. In order to reach him, however, Zarathustra must become ill and only then does he enter into his famous stage of convalescence that I have remarked on in the reading of Heidegger. Thus, 'downgoing' entails the search for a new image of thought that no longer assumes the form of 'critique', according to the Kantian image of critical philosophy; nor, I would argue, does it resemble Heidegger's 'closure of metaphysics', since it does not concern itself with the question of nihilism as the destination of the history of Western philosophy. Instead, as I will turn to demonstrate in Deleuze's own reading of the meaning of 'convalescence', it simply concerns a new conceptual persona of the philosopher invented by Nietzsche, particularly in *The Genealogy of Morals*, which is the conceptual persona of the philosopher as a diagnostician and pharmacologist. Concerning the latter, we should recall that the two greatest sources of illness espoused by all philosophy are 'reactive or bad consciousness' and 'a spirit of revenge against time'. In fact, these sources are actually described as two plants that have afflicted humanity with different states approximating intoxication, poison and hallucinatory delirium, and it is now only the conceptual personae of the new philosopher as diagnostician and pharmacologist that will be able to discern these toxic agents and prescribe a cure, one which leads to an actual recovery and health of the body and its drives (*animalitas*).

Before turning to the diagnostic image of thought in Deleuze's interpretation of 'convalescence' (namely, the period of sickness and recovery), I would like to call attention to one more detail concerning the claim of the concept. In Zarathustra, this claim is certainly understood as the claim to one concept, which is the concept of the Eternal Return; however, I would simply underscore the fact that this concept is nowhere presented or expounded by Zarathustra or any of the characters, nor certainly by Nietzsche himself, except that it is forecast as the most abyssal truth that stems from the consequences of the affirmation of the actual source of all values. In this regard, I would agree with Heidegger's closing remarks in his article that, although Nietzsche is able to propose this thought and have a presentiment of it as the highest peak of his own system, he is not able to fashion a concept of understanding that corresponds with the idea, and thus he lays out a field of immanence for the construction of the concept of the Eternal Return, but the actual concept nevertheless remains distant, remote, if not impossible to attain. Or, in Heidegger's own words:

> That Nietzsche experienced and expounded his most abysmal thought from the Dionysian standpoint, only suggests that he was still compelled to think it metaphysically, and only metaphysically. But it does not preclude that this

most abysmal thought conceals something unthought, which is also impenetrable to metaphysical thinking.[4]

In the above passage we can see how Heidegger's interpretation of Nietzsche's entire philosophy is split between the philosophical claim of a unique concept (in this case, the concept of the Eternal Return) and the identity of the conceptual persona who appears to present this claim 'from a Dionysian standpoint', which is Nietzsche's Zarathustra. According to Heidegger's interpretation, there is a distinction, even a suspense, found in Nietzsche's philosophy between the enunciation of this claim through the conceptual persona of Zarathustra and the failure to realise the concept in Nietzsche's philosophy, which can be said at that point onwards to belong to this philosophy, even though it remains 'unthought'. Of course, according to Heidegger's reading, this failure is not something petty, but rather says something great about Nietzsche's philosophy – that it belongs to a 'grand style' of philosophy, which also announces the direction of philosophy itself 'for tomorrow and the day after tomorrow', in the words of Nietzsche's own self-description. Heidegger understands this announcement via the conceptual persona of Zarathustra as the spokesperson and the teacher of the Eternal Return, and the conceptual persona of Zarathustra is merely a bridge on the way to the Overman (who, once again, appears nowhere in Nietzsche's philosophy). In other words, the Overman is the conceptual persona that unites three aspects of 'crossing over'. He is:

1. that from which the person passing over departs;
2. the bridge itself;
3. the destination of the person crossing over.

And yet, perhaps this is just another manner of portraying the temporal gap between the concept that is being claimed in Nietzsche's philosophy and the creation of the concept itself. Concerning the concept of the Eternal Return (which Heidegger reclaims as his own concept and thus the anticipation of his own philosophy), I am not the first to argue that this interpretation changes both the original destination as well as the orientation of Nietzsche's own philosophy. How does this orientation differ from Deleuze's interpretation of Nietzsche's philosophy?

It is at this point that I now turn to some passages from Deleuze's early interpretation to grasp the conceptual persona who appears as a diagnostician and a genealogist. As I have already claimed, the difference between the two readings comes down to how one understands the process of convalescence, or the experience of convalescing, which is the experience of suffering and illness that also expresses the image of health as the only possible resolution. It often happens that when I experience illness (for example, an intense migraine), I cannot remember the state of health that preceded it, but can only imagine the state that will follow which is marked by the absence of the present suffering. And yet, the absence of suffering is not the same thing as a feeling of health. Heidegger reads the meaning of this suffering as the low point of Zarathustra's journey, 'The Convalescent', after Zarathustra returns 'home' to the cave with his animals and falls into a deep intoxicated sleep. Therefore, he interprets suffering and pain as both 'homesickness' and 'longing', and the cause of the illness as 'revenge', and longing as 'freedom from revenge', which would provide us with a possible cure, or a path back to health.

According to my own interpretation, which I believe also complements that of Deleuze, I discern the suffering that leads to the stage of convalescence from the exact moment of its beginning, which occurs at the highest point of Zarathustra's journey, or at least a point where the directions of 'higher' and 'lower' no longer have any meaning since highest peak and deepest abyss have merged into one. Once again, this has to do with the source of the highest values and is presented in the form of a paradox in terms of Kantian philosophy. If, for Kant, the highest source of admiration and awe (i.e., the source of all theoretical values for philosophy) is 'the starry sky above me and the moral law within me', how then do we understand the reorientation of the highest source of values when they are suddenly turned upside down, since from the perspective opened in Nietzsche's philosophy in the figure of the Overman, the starry skies are now below and the moral law is no longer found within the subject of Man? With respect to Kantian critical philosophy, if the stars are indeed beneath me, then they no longer deserve the respect of my admiration and even awe, since they are in reality lower than Man, who is now responsible for populating the heavens as the expression of his will to power. But Kant was incapable of recognising this and succumbs again to a mystification, which becomes the source of the paradox between higher and lower values. In other words, the origin of the moral law is placed within Man, but in the form of an idea that is outside his power to grasp as a concept of the understanding, so that the origin of the moral law is just as unthinkable as the origin of the starry skies. But this is a pure fiction that is made to disguise the truth: it is the origin of the starry skies that is actually within me, since I alone am responsible for creating their unfathomable *height* in the first place, and then surrounding this act of creation with an air of mystery in order to hide this power from myself. What is this power except the power to create transcendental values?

At this point, let us turn to Deleuze's own reading of this moment, which appears in his *Nietzsche and Philosophy* at the beginning of the fifth section: 'The Overman: Against the Dialectic'. It is here we read the following sentence that confirms everything we said earlier concerning Zarathustra's abysmal thought:

> In the word nihilism *nihil* does not signify non-being but primarily a value of *nil*. Life takes on a value of *nil* insofar as it is denied and depreciated. Depreciation always presupposes a fiction: it is by means of fiction that one falsifies and depreciates, it is by means of fiction that something is opposed to life . . . The whole of life then becomes unreal, it is represented as appearance, it takes on a value of *nil* in its entirety. (NP: 147)

Immediately after this definition of nihilism, we find that it is the fiction of higher value itself that leads to the devaluation of life; it is the higher values themselves that lead to the depreciation of life, which are called 'symptoms', properly speaking. But the nature of the life we are speaking about here is not that of biological life, but rather the life that is expressed by will to power; thus the symptoms are the expressions of an active will to power that seeks revenge against life, or the *animalitas* of the living subject, which may or may not be identified with the deviation of *bios* and *zōe*, according to the interpretation of Agamben. In fact, it is the overturning of the previous orientation towards the highest of values, and the reactive consciousness of the lowest, that immediately becomes the source of a new suffering, which is the beginning of the period of the convalescence proper, which is why I have placed so much emphasis on the moment when Zarathustra says: 'I am ready, I begin my downgoing.' The ensuing period of suffering and illness is now understood to be caused by the 'downgoing' of all higher values and the metaphysical abstractions heretofore, but also by the question of the subject of knowledge who might be capable of discerning the source of the illness that has touched every value, both high and low, since this hierarchical distinction itself has been reduced to *nil*. It is the loss of all distinction that causes everything to become an abstraction, or to have its source in this abstraction, and at several points this sickness and this revelation fills Zarathustra with an unspeakable nausea that overcomes his body as well. This sickness is called a feeling of nihilism. But it is also at this point that a new conceptual persona emerges in the sense of giving to modern philosophy a new task of analysis and evaluation, the conceptual persona of the philosopher as critical diagnostician (or symptomatologist) and genealogical thinker, a thinker of poisonous roots and curative mixtures.

After coming to the precise image of thought that belongs to Nietzsche's philosophy, let us now return to the major statement of affirmation from which we began: every philosopher lays claim to a concept, but it is the conceptual persona who advocates for something by means of this concept. The diagnostician is the conceptual persona of the Nietzschean philosopher who lays claim to the concept of life, and who invents or creates concepts for life and on behalf of more life, and thus develops critical concepts in the sense of that they only have meaning if they produce this direction and goal. In other words, every diagnostician must already have an image of health and must produce this image alongside the critical concepts that designate the sources of illness or symptoms. It is this image of health that in some ways is encompassed in the Overman and what Deleuze calls Nietzsche's 'method'. As he writes:

> From this form of question there derives a method. Any given concept, feeling or belief will be treated as symptoms of a will that wills something. What does the one that says this, that thinks or feels that, will? It is a matter of showing that he could not say, think or feel this particular thing if he did not have a particular will, particular forces, a particular way of being. What does he will the one who speaks, loves or creates? (NP: 78)

What we need, as Nietzsche's philosophy can be heard to claim at many points, is a new image of health, which is to say, a philosophy that promotes life and which enters into combat with the opposite forces that wreak havoc on life, which have been promoted by all philosophies heretofore – not death, which is not proposed as the opposite of life, but rather 'revenge against life', a brutal domination of life, or 'bad consciousness' for which life itself becomes an affliction and a supreme cause of suffering. For example, freedom becomes 'freedom from suffering' that is attained by the form of right, according to the consciousness of the master, or by force of law, according to the consciousness of the slave – this is the concept of freedom that is expressed by bad consciousness. 'Bad consciousness' produces a race of masters as the highest men, whose will is essentially reactive in taking out their revenge against all lower forms of life. By contrast, slaves are simply masters who have learned to subjugate themselves and proclaim this as their highest value attained through a spirit of auto-subjugation (i.e., self-legislation). Of course, the concepts of both power and life are somewhat interchangeable in Nietzsche's philosophy under the notion of 'will to power', since the ultimate aim of any power is the creation or maintenance, or simultaneously the destruction or subjugation, of a certain form of life. Thus, the diagnostician enters in with his concept of life and an image of health, just as the genealogist of morals will appear two years later after Zarathustra with his concept of power and the forms of sovereign life it produces. As Deleuze writes:

> The kingdom of nihilism is powerful. It is expressed in values superior to life, but also in the reactive values, which take their place and again in the world without values of the last man. The question is: how can nihilism be defeated? How can the element of values itself be changed, how can affirmation be substituted for negation? (NP: 171–2)

This is the problem that Deleuze takes up in his reading of Nietzsche's philosophy, which again also 'prefigures' the conceptual persona of the genealogical method that follows from this problem and offers one possible method or solution. But how do we distinguish this genealogical method from that of the diagnostician and symptomatologist of the body that also represents another or accompanying method? If the source of the moral law formerly resided within Man, then Nietzsche will heretofore understand this to mean 'in his body', in the *animalitas* that has been repressed or denied by the creation of higher values to rule over all passions. Thus, 'The will to power is body, but what would we know of the body without the sickness which makes it known to us?' (NP: 172). Moreover, if indeed what was formerly called the 'starry skies above us' is the source of all our most theoretical and metaphysical abstractions, Nietzsche will also understand that the true origin of these abstractions have suddenly changed places and their source must now be discovered in the body. The diagnostician emerges to replace the doctor of metaphysics and to become a physician of the body defined by the relations between active and reactive forces. Here, we discover a new theoretical sense of wonder and awe that is now located in the body, which in some ways challenges the theoretical and speculative sense of wonder that was formerly ascribed to the starry skies above us. In fact, the human body is 'a more astonishing idea than the old soul' and 'one never ceases to be amazed at the idea that the human body has become possible' (NP: 204n). Here, I immediately turn to a passage that appears earlier in the section on active and reactive forces:

> What is the body? We do not define it by saying that it is a field of forces, a nutrient medium fought over by a plurality of forces. For in fact there is no 'medium', no field of forces or battle. There is no quantity of reality, all reality is already quantity of force. There are nothing but quantities of force in mutual 'relations of tension' . . . Every force is related to others and it either obeys or commands. What defines a body is this relation between dominant and dominated forces. Every relationship of forces constitutes a body; whether it is chemical, biological, social or political. Any two forces, being unequal, constitute a body as soon as they enter into a relationship. This is why the body is always the fruit of chance, in the Nietzschean sense, and appears as the most 'astonishing' thing, much more astonishing, in fact, than consciousness or spirit. (NP: 40)

According to a diagnostic method, what is called 'a body' is defined by a relation of forces that are always unequal, and constitute a hierarchy; therefore, 'a body' is composed only when these forces enter into relation with one another – whether we are speaking of a chemical relation, a biological entity, or a political or social aggregate of relations. As Deleuze writes, 'The birth of a living body is not really surprising since every body is living, being the "arbitrary" product of the forces of which it is composed' (NP: 40). Once one understands this simple law, then 'the body' (i.e., any body whatsoever, without distinction) is not so surprising and is no longer a source of mystery and abstraction. Moreover, it is from this basic understanding of the body composed by a relation of two or more forces that there can also be complex bodies in Nietzsche's philosophy, which have been formed by multiple forces because they extend over time and are historically shaped by forces that are no longer even active, but nevertheless leave their trace or mark (as in the case of consciousness, which has its degrees of unconsciousness).

This is the new image of thought proposed by Nietzsche's philosophy which derives its image from the three conceptual personae that Nietzsche's own philosophical construction and forms the three methods of what Deleuze calls an 'active science' no longer based on reflection or contemplation of the subject of reason. Deleuze cites the last note that appears in the edition of the *Genealogy of Morals*, which, as I have been arguing, he seems to privilege over the other works including *Thus Spoke Zarathustra*. As Deleuze writes, 'philosophy becomes symptomatology', since 'a phenomenon is not an appearance or even an apparition but a sign, a symptom which finds its meaning in an existing force' (NP: 3). Therefore, 'Only an active science is capable of interpreting real activities and real relations between forces':

> It therefore appears in three forms. A symptomatology, since it interprets phenomena, treating them as symptoms whose sense must be sought in the forces that produce them. A typology, since it interprets forces from the standpoint of their quality, be it active or reactive. A genealogy , since it evaluates the origin of forces from the point of view of their nobility or baseness, since it discovers their ancestry in the will to power and the quality of this will. All the sciences, including the sciences of nature, are brought together in such a conception, as are science and philosophy . . . When science stops using passive concepts it stops being a positivism and philosophy ceases to be a utopia, a reverie on activity which makes up for this positivism. The philosopher as such is a symptomatologist, a typologist, and a genealogist. We can recognise the Nietzschean trinity of the 'philosopher of the future': the philosopher-physician (the physician interprets symptoms), the philosopher-artist (the artist moulds types), the philosopher-legislator (the legislator determines rank, genealogy).

In short, according to a transvaluation of the activities of interpreting, classifying and legislating that even belonged to the previous philosophy, these are the three new conceptual personae of a 'philosophy of the future'.

Finally, at this point we must now ask: where is this future with respect to the present moment or what is called continental philosophy? Earlier on I said that the conceptual persona of Deleuze is an advocate for immanence over transcendence, in the sense that the entire philosophy can be heard at all times to advocate for this and to affirm this principle, which is more like a cry, as Deleuze says, than a proposition that could be proven either true or false. It is not even a belief in the usual sense of the term, which is predicated on the existence of something that can be qualified or doubted, but rather must be understood as the condition of all philosophical enunciation, even as an affirmation that is prior to every statement, to every negation or critical appraisal as well. It is for this reason that Deleuze himself does not even need to state it, or to prove it, and it is the silence that precedes or follows from every statement as both the logical condition of propositions and the ontological conditions of all statements. As Deleuze states concerning the image of thought that is presupposed by its conceptual personae, the question must always be renewed because the image of thought lives and dies only in the present and must constantly be renewed and filled with life again:

> After Lucretius how is it still possible to ask: what use is philosophy? It is possible to ask this because the image of the philosopher is constantly obscured. He is turned into a sage, he who is only the friend of wisdom, friend in an ambiguous sense, that is to say, an anti-sage, he who must be masked with wisdom in order to survive. He is turned into a friend of truth he who makes truth submit to its hardest test, from which it emerges as dismembered as Dionysus: the test of sense and value. The image of the philosopher is obscured by all his necessary disguises, but also by all the betrayals that turn him into the philosopher of religion, the philosopher of the State, the collector of current values and the functionary of history. The authentic image of the philosopher does not survive the one who can embody it for a time, for his epoch. It must be taken up again, reanimated, it must find a new field of activity in the following epoch. If philosophy's critical task is not actively taken up in every epoch philosophy dies and with it die the images of the philosopher and the free man. Stupidity and baseness are always those of our own time, of our contemporaries, our stupidity and baseness. (NP: 107)

In other words, philosophers must always lay out their concepts on a plane of immanence like throws of the dice that will be taken up (or not) both by their sympathetic listeners, but also by their greatest competitors – but especially their 'anti-pathetic' contemporaries who I will address below. In other words, to diagnose the contemporary image of thought we must also speak of our own stupidity and our own baseness as well. For example, in the opening paragraph of the conclusion of *Nietzsche and Philosophy* Deleuze speaks of his own contemporary moment with a Nietzschean scorn for what he calls the various scraps of modern thought:

> Modern philosophy presents us with amalgams which testify to its vigour and vitality, but which also have their dangers for the spirit. A strange mixture of ontology and anthropology, of atheism and theology. A little Christian

spiritualism, a little Hegelian dialectic, a little phenomenology (our modern scholasticism) and a little Nietzschean fulguration oddly combined in varying proportions. We see Marx and the Pre-Socratics, Hegel and Nietzsche, dancing hand in hand in a round in celebration of the surpassing of metaphysics and even the death of philosophy properly speaking. And it is true that Nietzsche did intend to 'go beyond' metaphysics. . . . We have imagined Nietzsche withdrawing his stake from a game which is not his own. Nietzsche called the philosophers and philosophy of his time 'the portrayal of all that has ever been believed'. He might say the same of today's philosophy where Nietzscheanism, Hegelianism and Husserlianism are the scraps of the new gaudily painted canvas of modern thought. (NP: 195)

2.

At this point, let us employ this new image of the conceptual persona of the philosopher as diagnostician to judge the equally gaudy portrait of so-called 'continental philosophy' today. So far, we have already established that the philosopher needs a conceptual persona in order to think, or rather, to speak while thinking. As we have seen in the case of Nietzsche's Zarathustra, the philosopher needs the intermediary of a conceptual persona to become the 'advocate' of his or her own image of thought, that is to say, a 'mouthpiece' or 'spokesperson' which functions differently from the narrator in a story or a novel, or the 'I' of the linguistic act. As Deleuze and Guattari write, 'in philosophical enunciation we do not do something by saying it but produce movement by thinking it through the intermediary of a conceptual persona' (WP: 64). Here we must distinguish between enunciation and mere speaking, for in the above passage 'enunciation' amounts to a 'movement in thinking' that refers to the agency of collective enunciation (*agencement collective*). For example, even after the individual philosopher falls silent and succumbs to either a natural death or ignominy – is there any other kind of death for a philosopher? – it is only his or her conceptual persona that can be heard to go on speaking, or rather, enunciating a movement of thought that once belonged to the living philosopher. It is in this manner that philosophers themselves become conceptual personae when their proper names begin to function more like common nouns such as 'Plato', 'Aristotle', 'Hegel' or 'Deleuze'.

We might ask whether this represents the same movement of thinking, or whether something has changed the form of enunciation? This question is important to ascertain those cases where the philosopher can no longer be said to be the agent of enunciation (i.e., the philosopher can no longer invent his or her own intermediary who says 'I'), and other agents (or 'actors') appear who emerge to speak in the place of the philosopher, which is to say, other interlocuters who will emerge either as the philosopher's sympathetic or antipathetic agents. It is not just the single or solitary philosopher who invents a conceptual persona, but rather a group of readers and commentators who follow (a bit like Zarathustra's animals), so that in the history of philosophy it is possible to say that there can be several personae for a single philosophy, given that 'each persona has several features that give rise to other personae', and thus, in this manner, the conceptual personae proliferate to represent a particular philosophy or philosopher (WP: 75). This means that what is peculiar to philosophy is the philosopher's need, in order to be able to communicate a movement of thought, to create a unique form of individuation, which does not refer to the personality or the psychology of the philosopher, but rather to something like an onto-genetic principle, or what Gilbert Simondon refers to as an 'outbreak of individuation', which often occurs through a special form of 'empathic identification' (*Einfühlung*) with the conceptual persona of a particular philosophy – for instance, Hegel for the Hegelians, Kant for the neo-Kantians, Marx for the Marxists, or Deleuze and the Deleuzians, Derrida and the Derrideans, Badiou and the Badiouians, and Žižek for just about everyone else.[5]

While I cannot pursue the sociological question concerning this form of individuation (including the question of whether philosophy necessarily remains bound to an Oedipal form of individuation and, thus, a masculine image of thought), one could point to the multiple forms of collective enunciation, or different 'molar individuals', that populate the field of contemporary philosophy today, especially the kind of philosophy that one most often finds on blogs or academia.edu. Nevertheless, what I am calling philosophical enunciation refers to a certain kind of movement: to think is to create a movement towards a plane of immanence (even if this movement simultaneously turns away), to affirm before negating, to construct, to lay out concepts, to partition, to divide up, to create), but this movement occurs only through the intermediary of a conceptual persona, and this operation is identified with the production of movement in thinking that simultaneously differenciates (*sic*) / is differentiated from other thoughts, other planes constructed by other philosophies. In order to demonstrate this, one only has to be reminded of Deleuze's statement concerning how certain philosophers have fundamentally changed what it means 'to think', and by doing so, how they not only reoriented a previous tradition of philosophical inquiry, or the 'history of philosophy', but also managed to establish the conditions of philosophical enunciation for every philosopher who came afterwards, who had to contend with their image of thought out of necessity, or run the risk of losing all reference to the name of philosophy itself in its most contemporary usage. For example, the name of Descartes no longer exclusively refers to the individual and does not function as a proper name, to the same degree that the term 'Cartesianism' does not refer only to Descartes's own writings but also to the tradition of philosophy that depends on his method as well as the antithetical philosophies that establish their image of thought on an essentially pejorative and negative usage of the same term. The theory of the proper name can be referred to Saul Kripke's causal understanding of the 'initial baptism' of the name as a referent (or 'rigid designator'), but must also be expanded to include 'subsequent baptisms'.[6] In the case of the name of Descartes, for example, we witness the birth of a distinctive, and yet historically changing, conceptual persona that appears to represent the philosophy of Descartes owing to multiple baptisms, in which the name functions both as a line of filiation and in a polemical sense of 'anti-Cartesianism'. Of course, everything I have just described can be applied to many other philosophers, both historical and contemporary – though not to all! – and what is most remarkable is the causal nature of certain philosophers who have produced such an extreme range of positive and negative evaluations. The volatile nature of specific conceptual personae becomes more dramatically evident in these special cases: Plato and Platonism, Descartes and Cartesianism, Spinoza and Spinozism, Kant and neo-Kantianism, Hegel and Hegelianism, Nietzsche and Nietzscheanism (and to this list we might also add several contemporary examples, including the philosophies of Bergson, Deleuze and, lastly, Derrida).

In each case, or for each conceptual persona listed by a 'rigid designator', the above history must also be accompanied by another series of conceptual personae beginning with the prefix 'anti-'. This especially concerns the antipathy that has developed at certain moments, as in the case of an 'anti-Hegelianism' that unites certain contemporary philosophies around a vague and indeterminate desire for something else, for another kind of movement of thinking that determines the future of philosophy. It is for this reason that perhaps there is an entire drama of attraction, repulsion, sympathy, empathy and antipathy that has also determined the conceptual personae of great philosophers, and which constitutes their becoming. This drama cannot be separated from the generalised struggle or agonism over the plane that a particular philosopher first produces as a movement in thought. As Deleuze and Guattari describe this becoming, 'conceptual personae carry out the movements that describe the author's plane of immanence, and they play a part in the very creation of the author's concepts' (WP: 63). Even when they are completely 'antipathetic', these conceptual personae belong to the plane that the philosopher in question lays out and to the concepts that he or she creates, also including the dangers specific to this plane. Besides, perhaps it is the philosopher who is also made responsible for all the bad perceptions, bad feelings and even negative movements that emerge from this plane, for they themselves first inspired these affective possibilities by proposing concepts whose repulsive character remains a constitutive property of that philosophy. For example, this is certainly true in the case of the philosophy of Nietzsche, and it may also be the case for Heidegger as well, but for different reasons and according to another mixture.

This introduces a feature of psychology into the creation of conceptual persona since the consciousness of the commentator (or 'secondary reader') must always be defined or diagnosed (as Deleuze would say, following Nietzsche) as a 'reactive consciousness'. This should not be understood negatively, since all consciousness is in a certain sense reactive, but simply as the physical condition that occasions the form of commentary to even exist, like the existence of a wave in the ocean: every commentator first feels that they have no body without organs of their own, and must borrow another more powerful body as the cause of saying 'I'. Otherwise everyone would be creating original philosophies – that is, everyone would be capable of producing an image of pure inorganic life, of fabricating their own body without organs. In the original encounter between consciousness and the body without organs, consciousness reacts to another more powerful body, with either acceptance or a spirit of revenge (what Nietzsche called the psychology of resentment). Of course, one of Deleuze's earliest works, *Nietzsche and Philosophy*, creates a diagnosis of the psychology of resentment as one of the most dominant traits in the history of Western philosophy. Therefore, in the history of philosophy, and in the history of all philosophical, literary and artistic commentary as well, one can immediately discern a spirit of resentment that disfigures and mutilates the original and more powerful body of the creator or the author, in order to separate this more powerful body from its own affects, its own expression, to turn it against itself, even to contradict its own statements, as Nietzsche often complained. Despite the appearance that many of these commentaries are often dressed up as the philosopher's most intimate friends and disciples, they often betray the original image of a non-organic life by turning it into a school or an academy. Once again, this is what Deleuze refers to as the double shame of 'the Scholar' and 'the Familiar', and concerns the feeling of shame concerning their own bodies, a shame that must be negated, disguised and displaced onto the reader, and this is what occasions the birth of the philosopher and his or her doubles.

It is also in this larger collective and social sense of empathy and antipathy (i.e., attraction and repulsion, bad feelings, negative perceptions, even failed becoming and abortive becomings) that the creation of a generic form of individuation becomes the condition of a generic multiplicity, or 'collective assemblage of enunciation'. Consequently, what one commonly refers to under the name of 'Deleuze' can also be defined in terms of the opposition to other movements, schools and other conceptual personae – in the sense that empathy breeds and is only sharpened by the forces of antipathy. From the early Greek to the contemporary moment, the history of philosophy is defined by these empathetic and antipathetic movements that become attached to a philosopher's name, and by a certain image or persona that stands for that thought, in the sense of constituting what is distinctive in this thought in contrast to all the others, and thus constitutes an original, even primitive, form of dramaturgy that originally belongs to philosophy. Although some might argue that it belongs more to religion, and to certain cultic forms of society bound up with the authority of a master, one must remember that philosophy also began as a cult and, in some ways, continues to assume this anachronistic social form up to the modern day. And yet, it is here, I believe, that one also discovers the social and collective resonance of what Deleuze and Guattari refer to as a special kind of empathy (*Einfühlung*), which allows philosophies to become collective and social movements of thought that come to be identified by souls thinking in a certain sense of moving together, forming a movement that occurs as much within a territory on the Earth as on a plane constructed by particular concepts and populated by conceptual personae. Beginning with the Greeks, and particularly since the dispersion of philosophies throughout Asia Minor in the Roman and early Christian periods, philosophies have gradually come to be identified as 'schools' (as movements, as collective societies, even as cults) and at the same time to begin to be differentiated by their conceptual personae: the Stoic, the Cynic, the Epicurean, the Neo-Platonist, even the Christian and the Jew. In Lucian's *Lives for Sale*, for example, these conceptual personae that stand for these different schools are often lampooned and parodied in a manner that was essential to understand the aspect of 'conversion' (metanoia) of all values and the guarantee of the best life that each school promised.[7]

So we must remark that the notion of the conceptual persona is not new to philosophy, or unique to Deleuze's or Nietzsche's philosophy, but in a certain sense represents the original social and collective dramaturgy of philosophy that in some sense Deleuze and Guattari sought to restore and reanimate – and precisely as a primitive and cultic form of individuation that can resist capitalist society, which is based on an axiomatic of identity. In the history of philosophy, it is perhaps Hegel who understood the nature of conceptual persona best and essentially modernised the original Greek sense of dramaturgy, which he recast in the form of the modern epic – thus spirit is shown dialectically to pass through all of its previous conceptual personae (Platonic, Stoic, Epicurean, Scholastic, etc.) until a stage of bad consciousness in which spirit strips away the dross appearance of all of its personae and appears for-itself, as the subject of self-legitimating reason. At this point, all the conceptual personae pass into history just as the figure passes through all its previous embodiments and genres and becomes identified with the mind itself, positing its thought in a universal form of writing – in the scientific form of the phenomenology. On the other hand, as I will return to below, it will be important to see how Nietzsche restores the original Greek and Christian dramaturgy with his conceptual persona of Dionysius, since spirit will be assigned again purely as an expression of the body and its passions.

For Nietzsche, however, the reader herself appears as a new conceptual persona who must be produced or willed alongside the creation of the author's conceptual persona for a philosophy of the future. She is not there from the beginning, but only belongs to the future and remains posthumous, or missing. As Deleuze and Guattari write, 'it is possible that the conceptual persona only rarely or allusively appears for himself. Nevertheless, he is there, and however nameless and subterranean he must always be reconstituted by the reader' (WP: 64). Therefore, it is the reader who leads us to the modern function of commentary as the favoured genre for the invention of new conceptual personae, and that has become the cause of both fame and ignominy for any modern philosopher, living or dead, and especially for those who have been fortunate or unfortunate enough to have been reconstituted by the prefix 'anti-'. One never begins to read a philosopher without confronting the shadowy presence of a conceptual persona who appears to obscure or block the primary work and, in some ways, to prefigure or even to pre-interpret it. Every philosopher is the lone figure at the back of the group, a figure preceded by a crowd of commentators; therefore, in reading a particular philosopher, one must always parry and struggle with the existence of the conceptual persona in approaching the philosophy and subtracting its too simple and clichéd image of thought with a more complicated and nuanced understanding. Perhaps, the best commentaries are those that manage to replace this conceptual persona with one of their own making, which is why I have previously argued that the function of commentators must be understood actually to write in the place of the primary philosopher, with all the ambivalence this act of substitution implies. This even explains why some of the best commentaries in the history of philosophy, like Deleuze's own, might at first appear to contradict and go against a common sense understanding or perception of the primary philosophy. In point of fact, all commentary must first 'defamiliarise', using the Brechtian term, or even 'destroy', employing Nietzsche's favourite word, an image of thought that has traditionally represented this philosophy, since they will later on explain how this image does not actually belong to the philosophy itself, but has been added later by a subsequent community of readers, a philosophical tradition, or by 'history itself', and must, subsequently, be subtracted or destroyed so that another image and a new conceptual persona could be erected in its place. Of course, there are also just as many examples of commentators who will function as 'false friends', secret rivals, including the unholy series of sorcerers, 'confidence men' and even tricksters in the history of philosophical commentary and secondary literatures. Therefore, in studying the creation of new conceptual personae, we must first acknowledge how so-called misinterpretations become extremely productive, even 'viral', over the course of time, and have sometimes even managed to determine the image of thought for centuries that follow, as in the case of Bayles's conceptual persona of 'Spinozism', which led in part to the Jacobi controversy.

At this point, we could provide many other examples from the history of philosophy, but I am more interested in the fate of contemporary personae. For example, among the many contemporaries to choose from, both Deleuze and Derrida could be singled out as haunted by the problem of their own conceptual persona. However, the existence of a dominant misinterpretation cannot simply be rationalised by referring to any species of error, as if the fate of interpretation amounted to a problem of simple mathematics, but rather must be explained in reference to the faculty of desire, which is why stupidity is not caused by error but addresses the capacity of freedom that is ascribed to the power of reason itself. As Deleuze first argued, the faculty of desire and the innate capacity of freedom determines the act of thinking that gives stupidity a moral dimension at its origin. It is also for this reason that the power of dissemblance that the conceptual persona produces in the place of all subsequent readings of a philosopher's work cannot be reduced to logical or hermeneutic error, since we know from experience that no amount of 'correct interpretation' can ever restore this image (and, God knows, many have tried, particularly in the case of Derrida). Instead, it is only by means of the invention of another conceptual persona (for example, another 'Derrida', a second 'Deleuze') who enters to do battle with the first, to overturn its image and steal the power of dissimulation itself (i.e., 'the powers of the false') – that is, to restore the effect of a pure simulacrum that can henceforth be judged as merely an extrinsic and external relation and no longer the expression of an internal genesis of thought with the identity of the thinker. For example, the entire problematic around the 'overturning of Platonism' refers precisely to this kind of battle and the need to invent a new conceptual persona, since in many ways the fate of a particular philosophy will be bound up with the good or bad nature of its conceptual personae.

It is because the entire history of philosophy can be described as a field of battle between different conceptual personae which are often designated by the same proper name or common noun that the entire problem of representation in philosophy can be better understood by referring again to the original sense of 'dramaturgy'. In attempting to grasp the original social meaning, in my own commentaries I have always been more interested in what happens to Deleuze's philosophy when it is read, translated, reproduced, adapted to other ends, but also when it is refuted, negated, opposed and often violently dismissed. In other words, I have always been more interested in all these events and misadventures, and perhaps this is why my work has been regarded more as literary criticism than philosophy, due to my intense curiosity and interest in the history of the reception of the philosopher's work, rather than in the total meaning of the philosophical system of concepts. As a literary critic, I understand that such a meaning is merely a 'figure in the carpet' whose secret desire is bound up with the commentator's fantasy of closing the book eternally, once and for all, as if to make the primary work redundant to the text of the commentary and no longer necessary, thereby internalising its external repetition in its own image of thought. Although the commentator often pretends to address the principal philosopher's work 'for the benefit of the readers' ('cc', or carbon copy – that is, two or more recipients of the original text), most commentaries speak 'in place of the philosopher', in the sense that they situate the subject of enunciation within the margins – and sometimes within the text – of the primary philosopher's writings in order to enunciate something that remains unsaid – to clarify and explain, to gloss or expand upon, correct or redact; to rebuke or erase, or to substitute the primary philosopher's language with their own. This gives to the art of philosophical commentary a very peculiar and often ambiguous subject of enunciation, as if there were the presence of a shadowy precursor and the signification of double entendre of stupidity (or blindness) and insight that underwrote every discursive situation belonging to this genre, since every commentary must first introduce a certain degree of stupidity into the work of the primary philosopher in order to be able to perform afterwards the arduous task of removing it like a splinter in the eye.

Perhaps it is for this reason that philosophers must always lay out their concepts on a plane of immanence like throws of the dice that will be taken up (or not) both by their sympathetic listeners and by their greatest competitors. Deleuze writes in *Nietzsche and Philosophy*:

> The authentic image of the philosopher does not survive the one who can embody it for a time, for his epoch. It must be taken up again, reanimated, it must find a new field of activity in the following epoch. If philosophy's critical task is not actively taken up in every epoch philosophy dies and with it die the images of the philosopher and the free man. Stupidity and baseness are always those of our own time, of our contemporaries, our stupidity and baseness. (N: 107)

Therefore, in judging the representation of contemporary philosophy, today we can only speak of our own stupidity and our own baseness. It seems we have no other choice than to select our own image of thought as 'the best', but in so doing we also fall prey to the same species of subjective illusion that Deleuze first sought to chase out into the open in both *Nietzsche and Philosophy* and, five years later, in the third chapter of *Difference and Repetition* on 'The Image of Thought'.

If the image of stupidity expresses a relation to an antagonistic desire that is the origin of a fundamental dissimulation of the sense that first belonged to the philosopher's own enunciation, then the democratising role of modern commentary has often been to replace the authority of the philosophical enunciation with an image of thinking that expresses a common-sense understanding, one that can also function socially to represent that philosophy in a nominative or accusative sense – for example, in the statements that one often hears, 'That's Spinozist' or 'Cartesian', 'That's Hegelian' or 'Marxist', 'Deleuzian' or 'Derridian'! Although these statements also function to socialise philosophy by bringing thought under the jurisdiction of dominant systems of judgement and value – and philosophy 'becomes' in this manner as well! – unfortunately, this also implies that the act of thinking itself is reduced to an image that does not think. Is this not, ultimately, a form of stupidity? Moreover, why would commentators desire such a thing in the first place, since it would appear to contradict and negate the meaning of their own activity, and risks turning it into a farce? Consequently, if I addressed the problem of stupidity above as a 'moral image of thought', following Deleuze's earlier argument, then perhaps its most appropriate genre is comedy or farce, and the creation of the conceptual persona in philosophy will be found to have an essential relation to the stereotype of the social persona in the comic form, the cliché in the linguistic form, and the dogmatic image in the moral form of thinking. These are the three forces or social forms of repetition and common sense that belong to the field of philosophy and define its semi-tragic battles and agonistic contests, as well as its comic figures and its public spectacles. Even today, when we hear someone speaking of 'Deleuzism', whether in a positive or negative sense, perhaps we are only witnessing a living drama by which even contemporary philosophy still reactivates the archaic conflicts of the original Greek *polis*.

Notes

1. Heidegger and Magnus , 'Who is Nietzsche's Zarathustra?'
2. See, especially, Lambert, *The Non-Philosophy of Gilles Deleuze* and *In Search of a New Image of Thought*.
3. Kant, *The Critique of Practical Reason*, 5:161.33–6, translated in Guyer, 'Introduction: The Starry Heavens and the Moral Law', p. 1.
4. Heidegger and Magnus, 'Who is Nietzsche's Zarathustra?', p. 431.
5. Simondon, 'The Genesis of the Individual'.
6. Kripke, *Naming and Necessity*, pp. 3–4.
7. Lucian, *The Downward Journey or The Tyrant*.

Part I:
'What is "continental" philosophy?'

1. Towards a Political Geology

Let's begin with an age-old question: if the earth had a philosophy, what would it be? Moreover, if the earth had a political philosophy, would it be a political theology, a new materialism or something more resembling a political geology? In taking up this question, first I will return to a very early pre-Socratic source: Hesiod's *Theogony*. Although some might immediately believe this to be a Western source, there are many Egyptian, Babylonian and northern African traces that are woven into the narrative, causing the mythic framework of the earth to become confused and contradictory. For example, in one of the original creation myths assembled by Hesiod, there is the story of the Earth (Gaia), and Heaven (Ouranos), and a certain progeny called Kronos (who is figured as the archaic forerunner of Chronos, or time). In this account it is said that Gaia is covered up by Ouranos, so much so that he never lifts his body from her day and night but constantly fornicates and pushes Gaia's progeny into the inner recesses of her body until, as the Greek puts it, Gaia is all 'crowded out', stuffed up with new generations to the point of bursting. It is at this point in the story that something strange occurs. A third party comes onto the scene, Kronos, who mysteriously is reported to be the first progeny of Gaia and Kronos – don't ask these stories to make sense, given that we must imagine that the first of Gaia's children escaped her eternal rape by Heaven and managed to slip away from the marriage bed of his two parents![1]

At this point it is reported that Gaia devised a 'crafty, evil device' (*techain*), or conspiratorial plot, with Kronos to rid her of her unwelcome suitor. She sent Kronos to hide behind a place of ambush (*loxos*, the ancient twin of *logos*), so that the next time Ouranos descended upon his mother, Kronos leapt from behind his place of ambush and castrated his father, which is why land and sky are divided in two from that point onwards so no part of Heaven actually touches the Earth. The original text reads:

All that came from Gaia and Ouranos, the most dire of children, from the beginning were hated by their own begetter; and just as soon as any of them came into being he hid them away and did not let them into the light, in the inward places of Gaia; and Ouranos rejoiced over the evil deed. And she, prodigious Gaia, groaned within, for she was crowded out; and she devised a craft, evil device . . . she sent him [Kronos] into a hidden place of ambush, placed in his hands a jagged-toothed sickle, and enjoined on him the whole deceit. Great Ouranos came bringing night with him, and over Gaia, desiring love, he stretched himself, and spread all over her; and he, his son, from his place of ambush stretched out his left hand, and with his right he grasped the monstrous sickle, long and jagged-toothed, and swiftly sheared off the genitals of his dear father, and flung them behind him to be carried away . . .[2]

If this act of separation was not terrible enough, the seed from Ouranos' bloody genitals and severed limbs was dispersed across the entire surface of Gaia's body. 'The drops of blood fertilize Gaia and generate Furies, Giants and Melian nymphs; the severed parts fall into the sea.'[3] It is from these seeds sprung the race of Titans (the bastard sons of Heaven), who would later assume the poetic figures the earthly powers, the monarchs and despots, the Caesars and, by extended analogy, the modern nations and territories. Although the last can only be prefigured allegorically in Hesiod's primitive fable, nevertheless we might see a modern map of the Earth pockmarked or tattooed with territorial nation-states and imperial colonies, and even the portrait of the return of Ouranos as the obese figure of globalisation, the giant colossus with two backs who lies a little too heavily on the Earth today. Moreover, it is because this new figure of Heaven appears more powerful and all-encompassing than Gaia's previous suitors that recently there has been a notable resurgence of mythic hope among the peoples for forging a new conspiracy with the Earth: either in the return of an archaic and bastard progeny to cut the genitals from this new colossus, or to locate in the body of the Earth itself a hidden and secret place of ambush. Basically, these could be seen as the allegorical figurations of the strategies or conspiratorial plots recently devised by political theologians and new materialists alike.

I do not recount this archaic fable of Greek theodicy here simply to be dramatic. In fact, one can find in the writings of Deleuze and Guattari a version, if not a revision, of Hesiod's fable in the description of the Earth whose body is said to be bloated ('trop gros'), pockmarked by territories, overburdened and weighted down by the despotic stratifications of sovereignty and the state, and especially the primitive *Urstaat* which is always just over the horizon of the historical strata. So many heavens have been invented to lie heavy on the Earth, like obese lovers that cover her body day and night; moreover, we might think of each heaven as the representation of a distinct stratum, and the multiple strata that pile on top of one another as the multiplication of layers or plateaus in the geological diagram that Deleuze and Guattari employ in their conception of 'stratification' as *the* problem of political geology, and of the Earth as suffering from too much stratification.

For example, we have the definition offered by Professor Challenger, a character drawn from the novels of Arthur Conan Doyle and Edgar Rice Burroughs, who first appears in *A Thousand Plateaus* to expound upon the concept of stratification.[4] According to Challenger,

> Strata are layers, Belts. They consist of giving form to matter, of imprisoning intensities or locking singularities into systems of resonance and redundancy, of producing on the body of the earth molecules large and small and of organizing them into molar aggregates. Strata are acts of capture, there are like 'black holes' or occlusions striving to seize whatever comes into their reach. They operate by coding and reterritorialisation upon the earth: they proceed by code and by territoriality. The strata are judgments of God; stratification in general is the entire system of the judgment of God (but the earth, or the body without organs, constantly eludes that judgment, flees and becomes destratified, decoded, deterritorialised). (ATP: 40)

A surface of stratification is defined as 'a more compact plane of consistency lying between two layers' (ATP: 40). But, as Deleuze and Guatarri also observe, 'strata always come in pairs', one serving as a substratum for the other. This can be readily illustrated in Hesiod's fable, with Gaia (Earth) forming the substratum of Ouranos (Heaven); however, something comes between them, the surface occupied by Kronos, the surface that exfoliates from the bloody genitals of Ouranos, which represents an original point of deterritorialisation which produces surface through which peoples and territories are first distributed.

It was only through the intervention of Kronos between this ancient pair of strata that the idea of an *externalized plane*, separated from the immediate joining of the two primitive strata, was first possible. The contradiction we have noted, the externalisation of the surface Kronos occupied as a place of ambush prior to the division of Earth and sky into two separate strata, can thus be interpreted as the retroactive image of the 'act' created afterwards as the necessary condition of its possibility. The original Greek meanings of *techain* (as plot, or secret pact between Gaia and Kronos) and *loxos* (a place of ambush, hidden away from Ouranos) also point to the political and strategic determination of a surface or place, even (non) place (utopia), from which the revolt against Heaven unfolded – that is, the two external relations to power or domination whose utopian meanings are obvious:

1. Conspiratorial plot or 'crafty device' invented by a revolutionary assemblage (or what Deleuze and Guattari will later call 'a war machine');
2. A utopian (non) place that constitutes the virtual point of emergence (or 'point of deterritorialisation') of new strata, and particularly those strata that concern us, which are composed of humans (but not exclusively, since they also include vegetable, mineral and even machinic phyla as well) and are defined less by species than by a distribution of strata that takes the distinctive form of a *socius*.

There are two types or organisations of the *socius* frequently discussed in *A Thousand Plateaus*: the primitive territorial-machine and the State-Form. From the perspective of the Earth (the immobile continuum, the ground of production, the body without organs), so-called 'human societies' appear only as over-coded blocks (either mobile or static), either organised into distinctive patterns of cities and territories, or more recently into mobile populations. The Earth is tattooed by the societies that emerge to represent the points of its surface that are over-coded. Moreover, humans do not appear 'on the surface', as they are attached to it by their organs (by their eyes, their hands, their mouths, their genitals, by their great and overdeveloped assholes) in order to make *another* meta-body. It is at this is point, as with Aristotle, where human beings cease to be defined primarily as biological entities and become elements of an entirely different assemblage called a *socius*, or 'social machine'. In turn, this creates the condition for the emergence of the great territorial machines that have distributed themselves across the surface of the Earth which have bodies of human beings as their parts, and their organs are now attached directly to the Earth through the intermediary of territorial signs, which are composed of matter drawn from the hybrid inscriptions of soil and blood. It is from these primitive territorial machines that the great races and the territorial bands emerge and strap themselves to the Earth's body like lines that crisscross the Dogon egg, carving out internal neighbouring zones, remote exterior precincts, frontiers and wastelands, boundaries and borderlines, and what Kant earlier described as the 'vast spaces of communication' (the oceans, deserts, the air) that lay between the doorsteps or portico of the *domus*, the homeland (*Heimat*), the native soil (*nation*).

Far from being a static notion, therefore, the concept of space that this process of stratification expresses is wildly productive. The specific characteristic of space that the processes of stratification expresses can be defined as a *vis activa*, by the tendency to proliferate and to multiply and become a 'manifold', something that Deleuze later on explores through the concept of 'the fold' (*le pli*). Throughout this process, however, the Earth must be defined as the *Thing* (*das Ding*) that remains consistent, immanently connected through all its points or surfaces (interior and exterior), or rather as a plane of consistency that becomes more compact and hardened the more strata or layers are produced. In other words, with each new surface actually produced through stratification, the Earth withdraws even further into itself, becoming more impenetrable and *In-Itself*. (I will return to comment on this tendency below when we return to the notion of 'deterritorialisation'.) Human societies can therefore be described as 'mega-machines' that cover the Earth – we recall the description of Ouranos, 'he stretched himself, and spread all over her' – and thus comprise its new surfaces of inscription and encoding. The question I have raised above concerns whether these surfaces can be arranged successively in a historical description, or whether their arrangement must be sought in the distinctive process of stratification itself.

The description of societies as 'mega-machines' requires us, once again, to clarify all this talk of machines in Deleuze and Guattari's writings. Following Louis Mumford, a 'machine' is actually a much more accurate manner of speaking of societies as, in fact, composed of the relations of production and surfaces of inscription (or what they call recording), that is, the relations of production and recording that are inscribed directly onto bodies which form the different surfaces of social machines. As they write: 'The social machine is literally a machine, irrespective of any metaphor, inasmuch as it exhibits an immobile motor and undertakes a variety of interventions: flows are set apart, elements are detached from a chain, and portions of the tasks are then distributed'

(ATP: 141). This description refers back to Marx's image of the relations of production that take on distinctive characteristics at each stage of the evolution of capital. Thus, 'it will be necessary to await capitalism to find a semiautonomous organization of technical production that tends to appropriate memory and reproduction, and thereby modifies the forms of the exploitation of man; but, as a matter of fact, this organization presupposes a dismantling of the great social machines that preceded it' (ATP: 141). Human societies are made up of lines, some of which are segmented and appear hard and easily noticeable on a surface of inscription-recording; however, others are more supple and appear further down (such as the flows of desire that are inscribed in the infrastructure of production itself), or take the shape of flows that circulate over the entire surface (flows of money, for example, that circulate in patterns that are difficult to perceive on first glance). There have been many different machines, as many as different organisations of the *socius* determined by the relations of production, from the primitive territorial machine, to the despotic feudal machines, to the machines of the nation-state, to the globalised machines of late capitalism. In each case, 'the flows are set apart, elements are detached, and tasks distributed'; however, in each case as well, new strata are produced that bear distinctive characteristics and new elements, which is why Deleuze and Guattari constantly emphasize the notion of 'territory' in distinguishing between different strata, or arrangements of the *socius*, in order to observe 'what has changed' in passing from one level, or stratum, to the next.

Nevertheless, it is only from the current perspective of this last machine that we can speak of the wholesale dismantling of all the machines that preceded it – thus, of the decline of the nation-state machine and its gradual incorporation into the machinery of global capitalism which today covers the Earth and constitutes a new surface of inscription and recording (or global memory), and which unites all events and bodies into one *mega-machine* at 'the end of History'. This is why Deleuze and Guattari often claim that capital is perhaps the most 'miraculous' of all previous social machines, since it appears that everything that happens has been preordained to happen to bring it into being and to make it the internal and genetic presupposition of every previous *socius*. As Deleuze once remarked: 'The first capitalists are waiting there like birds of prey, waiting to swoop down on the worker who has fallen through the cracks of the previous system. This is what is meant by primitive accumulation' (DI: 268). And yet, this is an illusion that belongs to the 'History of Capitalism' itself – that is, to the idea of universal history which is completely consistent with the encoding of capital and its specific line of development onto the full body of the Earth, of the process of stratification in which it plays the role of an *Urstaat* that organises every other social form that preceded it, even those that are remote in time or place, and some that have yet to be invented ('the most ancient and the most recent forms of exploitation of man by man') (ATP: 140).

Following the observations made by Maurice Godelier, Deleuze and Guattari argue against what could be understood as the underlying theoretical assumption that belongs to the current thesis of globalisation: rather than the West's line of development being universal because it recurs everywhere else, it must be understood as universal because it has recurred nowhere else; 'it is typical therefore [only] because, in its singular process, it has obtained a universal result.'[5] To describe the category of the 'universal' as 'typical', or general, is very different from saying it is determining 'in all cases'. (This recalls the problem of logic based on syllogism.) On the other hand, many current theories of globalisation (including, the current theories concerning neoliberalism) continue to mistake the two types, or species of universality, which can be defined in terms of the necessity, rather than contingency, of the Western line of development. Why is it, one might ask, that the most critiques of the capitalist system insist on the universality of the first kind, that it has and will continue to recur everywhere else according to the line of development first established in the West, rather than developing the critical insight that its form of universality corresponds to a line of development that belongs to the West and 'could recur nowhere else'? In other words, the more that the current critiques of capitalism continue to 'universalise', the more they pretend to speak from the position of the full body of the Earth, the more they continue to perpetuate the myth of globalisation according to one line of development defined as a process of stratification that encodes the entire surface of the Earth – *that stretches itself, and spreads all over her*! In fact, the *singular universality* that belongs to the Western line of development is expressed in the form of *absolute imperium* that characterises its political organization of democratic states, but all along a line of a singular interest that must find its own limit 'at a certain point' in other organisations that are always located 'outside' the West.

For example, one cannot say that the current line of development of capitalism in China belongs to the same line of development one finds in Europe or America – at least, not without reducing the 'deterritorialisation' of globalised markets that the Chinese economy has produced today – and often this results in yet another appeal to the universality of the Western line of development as determining the conditions of stratification in other regions, which is simply the early model of centre and periphery applied to multiple places across the globe. In this regard, it is interesting to recall that the line of development that almost exclusively preoccupies Hardt and Negri's appropriation of the narrative of 'Universal History' in *Empire* is the Western form of *absolute imperium*. However, as Deleuze and Guattari write,

> if we say that capitalism determines the conditions and the possibility of a universal history, this is true insofar as capitalism has to deal essentially with its own limit, its own destruction – as Marx says, insofar as it is capable of self-criticism (at least to a certain point: the point where a limit appears, in the very movement that counteracts this tendency). (AO: 140)

In this regard, we might determine that the problem of 'the West' is, in a certain sense, equivalent to the problem of 'Oedipus' in Deleuze and Guattari's earlier argument, that is to say, as a form of universality that captures desiring-production, recoding all deterritorialisation according to its own singular axiom. Accordingly, 'The West' produces the *universal* as its own 'plane of immanence', and then 'rejoices over the evil deed' (Hesiod).

As Deleuze and Guattari argue, moreover, it is only from the perspective of the full body of the Earth (or 'the absolute point of deterritorialisation') that the idea of 'Universal History' can first appear not only as 'retrospective' (with respect to the Western line of development), but also 'contingent, singular, ironic and critical'. This remark is important with regard to the possible manners in which capitalism may encounter its own limit 'outside' or 'beyond the line' of its own internal development, and specifically the development of Western capitalist societies. In some sense, the limit in question concerns the appearance of its universality when viewed from the perspective of other societies, which could only appear as 'contingent, singular, ironic, or critical' – in other words, as finite arrangements of interest that always flow back to 'the West'. Hence, the critical remark made by Grodelier above is extremely important for perceiving how the form of juridical sovereignty that underlies Western democratic institutions and ideas – and the idea of the universal especially – has functioned as the immobile motor of the expansion of the Western line of development in the form of *absolute imperium*. As

Grodelier observes, even the theoretical idea of socialism (developed, in part, in compensation for the forms of exploitation that belong 'retrospectively' to 'the History of Capitalist Societies') now confronts other societies and 'cause[s] them to leave behind the most ancient as well as the most recent forms of exploitation of man by man'.[6]

And yet, here we might ask: *to leave them behind for what?* The new forms of exploitation that belong to technical process of the production of capital, and for the benefit of 'a new impudent race of Masters' (Deleuze) and alongside the creation of new exploited classes that populate the different regions of the Earth today? This is what Grodelier refers to as 'the authentic universality of the West's line of development'. However, we should only accept this remark as ironic and critical, since it shows how the 'authenticity' of Western notions universality (but also notions of social justice, equality, fraternity, etc.) are appearing more externally from the perspective of non-Western societies in light of the difference from the actual practices of Western democracies. Therefore, it is not by accident that the most recent critiques of capitalist societies have been reoriented around locating a critical limit that is internal to capital itself, that is, to developing their analysis from a position of immanence internal to the history of capitalism itself, rather than from the perspective of external synthesis of the State-Form. This even forms a certain *sensus communis* that many theories today all share in common, having benefited from Deleuze and Guattari's earlier intuition that the most critical relation to capitalism is not external, but is rather immanent to capitalist processes of encoding desire directly at the level of bodies.

As Deleuze has argued, 'what matters is not ideology, nor even the "economic/ideological" distinction or opposition; *what matters is the organization of power*. Because the organization of power, i.e., the way in which desire is already economic, the way libido invests the economic, haunts the economic and fosters the political forms of repression' (DI: 263). In other words, this is also what Deleuze and Guattari suggest by the statement that capitalism must 'deal with its own limit, its own destruction', and this would occur precisely at those points where its own 'authenticity' is constantly being placed in crisis. This occurs where its expression of universal history appears against the background of its difference from other lines of development, and in the realisation that its own particular idea of universal history could reoccur nowhere else, and thus would no longer cause other societies to 'leave behind' the forms of exploitation of man by man. Such is already the case in different regions of the world and in certain 'other societies' where there is a preference for the return of 'primitive territorial machines' (e.g., the so-called 'Oriental line of development', or the archaic imperium of Islamic fundamentalism) over the adoption of 'Western ideas', including the ideas of democracy, socialism and communism. Political and economic theorists have already perceived that the history of capitalism in the West is contingent on a certain line of development, one that is completely dependent on *expansion*, that is, on 'immobile motor of deterritorialisation' and a process of stratification that displaces the limit internal to the capitalist *socius* onto different segments of the Earth and, in particular, to always confront this same line in the 'other societies' it encounters and in the new forms of exploited labour that it has created in its attempt, as Marx said, 'to go still further'.

At this point I recall the critical diagnosis of this tendency that is offered by Deleuze from the 1973 interview 'Capitalism and Desire':

> In every respect, capitalism has a very particular character: its lines of escape are not just difficulties that arise, they are the very conditions of its operation. Capitalism is founded on a generalized decoding of every flow . . . It did not create any code; it created a kind of accounting, an axiomatic of decoded flows, as the basis of its economy. It ligatures the points of escape and moves ahead. It is always expanding its own borders, and always finds itself in a situation where it must close off new escape routes at its borders, pushing them back once more. It has resolved none of the fundamental problems. It can't even foresee the monetary increase in a country over a year. It is endlessly recrossing its own limits, which keep on appearing farther out. It puts itself in alarming situations with respect to its own production, its social life, its demographics, its periphery in the Third World, its interior regions, etc. *The system is leaking all over the place.* (DI: 270; emphasis mine).

Deleuze and Guattari constantly emphasise that it is the very same principle of deterritorialisation upon which this form of capitalism depends as its 'immobile motor' that has always haunted each society in which it historically appeared as the terrifying nightmare from which it cannot awaken. This is because in each instance of deterritorialisation that allows the capitalist *socius* 'to displace its own limit further out, and to move on' (across the surfaces of the Earth), there always appears a frightening tendency of this process to veer towards a point of 'absolute deterrititorialisation'. In this context it is important to observe that Marx in the *Grundrisse* first adopted this image of absolute deterritorialisation in order to portray the successive transformations of capital itself, which purportedly always encounters its own limit as the inherent condition of its evolution and historical transformation, all the way to the end when this limit will potentially become externalised in a new form. That is, if there is a necessary limit internal to capital itself, which functions both as the condition of its production and reproduction and as the moment when capital exhausts itself and 'turns about' into another form (that is, the moment of *crisis*), it is a limit it had to *steal* from the Earth in the first place – as the absolutely *In Itself! the immobile continuum! the ground of all desiring-production!* This produces an extremely peculiar, if not 'singular', expression of *dread* that can be found at the basis of Western religious, sexual (or familial), political and philosophical institutions: specifically, the dread of 'decoded flows'. In fact, the more that the West has expanded by displacing its own interior limit onto the full body of the Earth, the more vulnerable the Western societies have become 'to a dread they feel for a flow that would elude their own code', a strange feeling of dread that has returned in the heart of all of all its social institutions.

In the mid-1980s, Lyotard speculated on the apotheosis of this 'absolute limit' in a series of reflections on the posthuman, where he posits the explosion of the Sun and thus the extinction of our solar system in around 4.5 billion years from now. 'That's not a question,' he writes. 'While we talk, the sun is getting older. It will explode in 4.5 billion years. It is [now] just a little beyond its expected lifetime' (I: 8). In other words, that the Sun will explode is thus posed as a 'fact' and, as Lyotard writes, 'there won't be a thought to know that its death took place' (I: 9). In other words, the very apparition of a limit (or finitude) that has determined and oriented terrestrial thought from the beginning has changed sense and meaning – as he says, 'even death would no longer be the right word!' – since with 'the death of the sun' thought will have stopped too, 'leaving disappearance absolutely unthought of' (I: 9). As Lyotard concludes, moreover, 'in 4.5 billion years there will arrive the demise of your phenomenology, and your utopian politics, and there'll be no one there to toll the death knell or hear it' (I: 9).

With this apocalypse, Lyotard posits the identity of thought and the human, and binds that human and all other biological life to an earthly existence, so our species is also bound to this absolute limit from which thought (called science) borrows from the Earth a limiting horizon and orientation *against* the infinity of matter that knows only endless change.

In other words, we would not be able to conceive of a purely material-ist (scientific) point of view – to incorporate it into our thought as a factical horizon of matter itself – if our species was not haunted from the beginning, as if the absolutely exterior limit of matter did not also concern our bodily existence (the essential element of sensory, cognitive and emotional experience to which all thought is inextricably indebted), which constitutes the source of the singular finitude that we also share with other terrestrial life forms.

According to Lyotard's most striking and original thesis, nevertheless, it is precisely this limit that we seek to negate by extending the possibili-ties of the human beyond our corporeal and earthly existence in order to, in the end, survive the death of the Sun. This requires a thought that longer needs a body, that no longer is bound to that limit, a form of thought in which energy is converted into information and reconverted into new matter. In other words, we are in the evolutionary process of leaving our bodies behind – which requires, first of all, that our bodies become more accessible by knowledge and technology – in order to be able to leave the Earth behind as well. With the evolution of cybernetic systems and artificial intelligence, the process of increasing complexity will also involve converting the former limits into knowledge and infor-mation along with the invention of a subject who is capable of process-ing information effortlessly. This has been going on for some time in the earlier cybernetic theories and informatics that were premised upon the redundancy of the biological substrate (i.e., the human body), and thus the gradual replacement of carbon-based consciousness by silicon life-forms as in the recent invention of AI. As Lyotard already observed much earlier, 'this and this alone is what is at stake today in technical and scientific research in every field from dietetics, neurophysiology, genetics and tissue synthesis (bioplastics) to particle physics, astrophysics, cybernetics, information science and nuclear physics' (I: 12).

It is not merely accidental or spurious, moreover, especially in the last century with the advent of the technological age, that this absolute limit often appears in the social and political phantasies that depict the 'end of capitalism' as an event that is equal to the end of the Earth. For example, let us imagine that tomorrow the Sun explodes or that the Earth is struck by a giant meteor that extinguishes all biological life and every *socius* distributed across its full body. The true question would be whether the Earth itself would ever even notice this as an event, but would remain absolutely indifferent, the immoveable, and glacial

entity that has terrified every society trembling on its surface? Would
the Earth be concerned whether the life forms that occupied its body,
be that of a human *socius* or, to employ a beautiful phrase first coined by
Jonathan Schell in *The Fate of the Earth*, merely a 'Kingdom of insects and
grass', or even if someday the Earth returned to a purely mineral environment without atmosphere or vegetable life? Would this not be one
way of imagining 'the end of capitalism'? Moreover, can we not detect
a strange mixture of desire and dread in the recent strategies of both
speculative realism and new materialism to erase the limit of human
finitude from the condition of thought itself, that is to say, to convert
the limit into the infinity of matter and energy in an endless exchange
and reconversion without any entropy in either thought or desire (i.e.,
endless desiring production, body without organs). Does this not imply a
more contemporary version of the same fable from Hesiod concerning a
new conspiracy with the Earth?

Here, I return to the question of why we are in the process of erasing
the former limit, the so-called 'subjective' limit of the human, if not to
prepare consciousness to be capable of greater and multiple degrees
of complexity. But the question becomes why this erasure of the limit
that also involves our bodies and our very openness to the event of time
and temporality, to the unknown Thing in itself, is negated in favour of
becoming knowledge – that is, information that can easily be recalled or
reproduced to effectively control time and avoid the event that, in the
older phenomenology, was called 'death'. But why is this posed in terms
of liberation of the subject for something else – or in favour of someone
thing else that is 'inhuman'? Is this because, according to Lyotard, 'the
human race has to now "dehumanize" itself, in the sense that it is still
too much a bio-political species, in order to rise to a new level of complexity, "so as to become tele-graphic"' (I: 53)?

Finally, this raises a crucial point that Deleuze and Guattari have
continued to make in their work – that the end of capitalism (or 'the end
of history', as the dominant myth that belongs to capitalist societies) is
not and has never been the most critical limit to achieve. 'Every civiliza-
tion and every epoch have had their ends to history. It's not necessarily
insightful or liberating. The moments of excess, the celebrations, are
hardly more reassuring' (DI: 266). And it is not by chance that contemporary popular culture is replete with fantasies concerning the end of
the world, from *Independence Day* to *Armageddon* and the *Terminator* and
Matrix series. Ironically, we are always having the same collective dream

– 'the end of capitalism' – Neo-Marxists and Neo-Conservatives alike! Otherwise, how do we account for the universality of this collective fantasy except that it issues from the dread that already determines the internal limit of the capitalist *socius* itself, but a dread that is recorded on bodies by culture as expressions of desire, jubilant intoxication, delirium and moribund fascination. For Deleuze and Guattari, it is the Earth ('the body without organs', or 'the Deterritorialised, the Glacial, the Giant Molecule') that provides us with the glimpse of the absolute limit! If anything, one sees from the perspective of this limit a supreme and terrifying indifference to the 'end of history', if not the fundamental image of terror itself, which is nothing less than the petrifying face of the death drive. *NOTHING! ABSOLUTELY NOTHING!* This, in my view, is what the Earth thinks about the contemporary *socius* that is tattooed across a surface of its full body, and which after all, is only a very temporary and minor skin disease.

To conclude, let's now return to our original question: if the Earth had a politics, what might it be? Certainly, following Deleuze and Guatarri, of course the answer would be a politics of 'deterritorialisation'. A politics of Gaia–Kronos. Or perhaps the politics of Speranza–Friday.[7] However, we must return to make one small correction. It would appear from the illustration offered above that the Earth can simply be defined as a primitive stratum, perhaps even the first or the 'original stratum'. On the contrary, Deleuze and Guattari do not define the Earth as a stratum, 'original' or otherwise, but rather as a more compact plane of consistency that lies between layers or strata. 'In effect, the body without organs [which has already been identified as the Earth in the earlier passage cited above] is itself the plane of consistency, which becomes compact or thickens at the level of the strata' (ATP: 40). This is how they avoid the charges of a 'return to Nature', as if they were saying that the plane of consistency (including the consistency of desire) is a 'natural state' that exists prior to the moment of stratification which causes it to deviate from its true unitary composition or to become 'outside itself within itself'. This would just be an inverted Hegelianism, and perhaps we were led astray here by the moral associations of rape in the story of Hesiod. There is always a danger in using fables (or 'fictions') in explicating concepts, which are made up of lines and not of images, and which is why we need to restore a proper degree of abstraction to the image of the Earth offered earlier on.

From our earlier description, we seem to have two mutually exclusive propositions in defining the Earth. On the one hand, it is defined as 'absolute deterritorisation', and Professor Challenger already described the Earth, or the body without organs, as what constantly 'flees and becomes destratified, decoded, deterritorialised'. On the other hand, the Earth has also been defined as 'the plane of consistency that thickens and compacts between strata'. This would appear to be contradictory only if the movement of deterritorialisation was always opposed to formations of congealment or stratification (or what Deleuze and Guattari call 'reterritorialisation'). But, as they write: 'Absolute deterritorialisation is not defined as a giant accelerator; its absoluteness does not hinge on how fast it goes. It is actually possible to reach the absolute by way of phenomena of slowness and delay' (ATP: 56). Consequently, thickness and density also resist stratification, as much as a surface that is characterised by dispersion and by externalised elements, and we might imagine that deterritorialisation must also be figured as those points that are impermeable and infinitely dense that can occur within any strata, forming 'black holes' or points where the Earth becomes too dense and undifferentiated. In each case, the process of stratification fails to 'capture' matter and transform it into a surface of encoding; the Earth no longer functions as a 'substratum' but comes undone and goes adrift, or reappears 'outside' the strata themselves, but this is only an illusion caused by the failure of its particular matter to be articulated by the process of stratification.

The point of all this is, again, to be discovered in the thesis of Professor Challenger: that the Earth absolutely resists all stratification, eludes and becomes deterritorialised, always veering towards a point of 'absolute deterritorialisation', and it is this degree of resistance that appears in the residues that constitute the relative and varying degrees of deterritorialisation that belong to the strata themselves. Thus, absolute deterritorialisation (the Earth) appears twice, or is doubly articulated, and 'appears relative only after stratification occurs on that plane or body' (ATP: 57). This is why, according to Deleuze and Guattari, 'there is a perpetual immanence of absolute deterritorialization within relative deterritorialization', and why 'the plane of consistency [the Earth] is always immanent to the strata' (ATP: 56–7). Returning to apply this insight to the fable by Hesiod, the Earth must be figured as both a 'prisoner to stratifications, and enveloped in a certain specific stratum that defines its unity of composition' (Gaia) and, at the same time, as that 'most unformed, destratified element that belongs to its plane of consistency' (Khronos). This removes any remaining hint of naturalism from Deleuze and Guattari's geophilosophy, since the Earth can only be defined as the mobile continuum between two states of deterritorialisation, the plane of consistency that appears between relative and absolute deterritorialisation or as the tipping point that causes one state to pass into another. But again, the strata themselves are only residues of these passages from one state to another, which is why they are constantly haunted from within by the movements of relative deterritorialisation that always threaten to become absolute.

The Earth can only be defined by this degree of imbalance, or disequilibrium, in the same way that any surface of stratification (of territory, or the stratified surface of the Earth under capitalism) is always found to be animated by deterritorialised and decoded flows; this is Deleuze and Guattari's thesis concerning capital, for example, which is said to be 'leaking everywhere' and 'endlessly crossing its own limits', which it keeps pushing farther out. At the same time, it is precisely through this fact that it is always expanding its own borders, as Deleuze argues, and 'always finds itself in a situation where it must close off new escape routes, and push them back' into its own body (DI: 270). Thus, if the couple formed by Gaia–Ouranos would form one image of the Earth (in which the Earth is shown to expand by internalising all strata into her bloated body), then the couple figured by Gaia–Khronos could provide another image (in which the Earth suddenly exfoliates all its strata on a surface that has no unity, but is characterised by an essential dispersion). And yet, these two images would not be opposed to one another, since one would form the internal presupposition of the other in the same way that every movement of deterritorialisation produces the conditions for reterritorialisation, recoding or new stratifications, and every reterritorialisation always foresees new possibilities of deterritorialised flows and even takes steps in anticipation of these flows and seeks to capture them, and to internalise them once more. But in each case, these possibilities appear as unprecedented and take on new character and new revolutionary potential. As Deleuze said: 'So, you see, there is hope' (DI: 270). This would be the hope of causing one state to pass into another, without going too far, of tipping the Earth over and causing it to spill out onto another plane of consistency, which would the critical perspective of geophilosophy. Is there a possibility of a new conspiracy with the Earth, one that would be different than the old paranoid conspiracies of 'totalisation' and 'overdetermination'?

If, as Deleuze once observed, the philosophy of the future must become a species of science fiction, then this trait would be even more pertinent to characterise a geophilosophy, or a philosophy of the Earth. It is for this reason that it cannot take the form of a political theology, since its concepts are unfolded on a ground that knows nothing of transcendence, but only of an 'outside' that is much older than history. But what of desire or power, the composition of the strata, the inevitable processes of stratification? The question of empire? If such questions could be asked any longer, it would only occur further down, well beneath the surface, congealed and hardened at some distant level of the interior stratum. Perhaps it will have become the question of anthropologists and natural historians, but not of politics, for that is a question that is always reserved for the surface, and I imagine this will be just as true then, as it will be in the future. The most critical point of view is only achieved in thinking of surfaces, in terms of which surface we occupy now or the one emerging just next to us, and not in terms of 'the culture of memory' that belongs either to the past or the future, since 'revolution has nothing to do with an attempt to inscribe oneself in a movement of development and in the capitalization of memory, but in the preservation of a force of forgetting and a force of underdevelopment as properly revolutionary forces' (DI: 278). Deleuze and Guattari have often referred to Marxism as a 'culture of memory', one whose theoretical practice always proceeds by the 'capitalization of the memory of social formations' (DI: 278). As I have argued throughout, this would have to be distinguished from the theoretical practice proposed by their notion of 'geophilosophy', which proceeds through the cultivation of a force of forgetting that they already find in the processes of deterritorialisation and reterritorialisation, and in the example of the Earth. According to a science of political geology, the future is not a surface that unfolds deep within the strata. Rather, the future is an egg and the earth, as Deleuze and Guattari have remarked many times, does not have a future, but rather a 'becoming' (or many becomings), for better or for worse. 'What does the Earth think it is becoming now?' is perhaps the only critical question that remains on our contemporary horizon.

Notes

1. Kirk and Raven note that the details of Hesiod's version suggest that Ouranos did separate from Gaia, 'at least in the daytime', but it 'is

probable that in other versions of the story Ouranos covered Gaia day and night (as Rangi covers Papa in the Maori myth), so that in a manner of speaking "the sky and earth were one form"' (Kirk and Raven, *The Pre-Socratic Philosophers*, p. 35).

2. Ibid.

3. Ibid.

4. In addition to his better-known Tarzan novels, Burroughs created a series of novels in which a scientist and an adventurer travel by mechanical machine through the Earth's crust to find another earth, ringed inside the Earth's core with its ball of fiery plasma as a secondary sun, which is called Pellucidur. Whether or not this allusion was conscious on Deleuze and Guattari's part, I am assuming that their invention of Professor Challenger is based on the hybrid fictional character of the nineteenth-century geologist-explorer of the Earth's strata.

5. Gondelier, quoted in ATP: 140.

6. Grodelier, quoted in ATP: 140n.

7. Deleuze's early reading of Michel Tournier's novel *Vendredi, ou les Limbes du Pacifique* echos, in an uncanny manner, the original fable by Hesiod and ends with the Speranza (the Earth) being emancipated from the 'sad sexual economy' of Robinson Crusoe, the global personification of European colonisation, an event which is brought about by the figure of 'Friday' (LS: 301–20).

2. The Question: 'What is "continental" philosophy?'

In pursuing a geopolitical image of thought, I now take up a question that has been asked many times over the past forty years. It is a cousin of the more classical question that is the title of Deleuze and Guattari's last work, but is related more like a bastard or orphan child of the original patronym: 'What is "continental" philosophy?' Traditionally, this question has been posed according to the analytic versus continental divide, but this division is an improper syllogism, and has become more and more simply the product of a disciplinary order of reproduction belonging to academic philosophy in the UK and the United States. As the late Gary Gutting has written on this opposition:

> The distinction between analytic and continental philosophers seems odd, first of all, because it contrasts a geographical characterization (philosophy done on the European continent, particularly Germany and France) with a methodological one (philosophy done by analyzing concepts). It's like, as Bernard Williams pointed out, dividing cars into four-wheel-drive and made-in-Japan. It becomes even odder when we realize that some of the founders of analytic philosophy (like Frege and Carnap) were Europeans, that many of the leading centers of 'continental' philosophy are at American universities, and that many 'analytic' philosophers have no interest in analyzing concepts.[1]

It would not be difficult to determine the historical origin of the opposition between so-called continental and analytic camps, which can actually be dated back to Bertrand Russell's vituperate remarks concerning the popularity of Bergson's philosophy in the 1920s in preference for the logical philosophy of Wittgenstein. Russell went on public record as early as 1908 in condemning Bergson as a false prophet and 'transcendental mystic', and, as Mary Ann Gillies and Ann Banfield have both argued, his suspicions around Bergson's popularity could be understood as a motive for his role in promoting the *Tractatus*, and Wittgenstein's precise vision of logical philosophy, as a new gospel. For Russell this is owed to a strong suspicion concerning the emphasis of imagination and the sense of sight in Bergson's concept of intuition and creative imagination, which would make it more disposed to a popular taste. It is not by accident that Bergson's translator and greatest early follower in the English-speaking world was the critic and Imagist poet T. E. Hulme, even though he also recanted his earlier association in view of the popularity of Bergsonism among the masses.

Although their choice of methods were different, the one trait that both Bergson and Wittgenstein shared is the hatred of a traditional language of metaphysics, and a tendency to either radically limit this language by submitting it to destruction through the revelation of contradiction – as Wittgenstein wrote 'I destroy, I destroy, I destroy!'[2] – or, in the case of Bergson, to replace the relative viewpoint and the dependency on the symbol with an urge for creativity and an intuition of the Absolute.[3] As he wrote in the 'Introduction to Metaphysics' (1903):

> A comparison of the definitions of metaphysics and the various conceptions of the absolute leads to the discovery that philosophers, in spite of their apparent divergences, agree in distinguishing two profoundly different ways of knowing a thing. The first implies that we move round the object; the second that we enter into it. The first depends on the point of view at which we are placed and on the symbols by which we express ourselves. The second neither depends on a point of view nor relies on any symbol. The first kind of knowledge may be said to stop at the relative; the second, in those cases where it is possible, to attain the absolute.[4]

While the tradition of continental philosophy has continued along the modernist impulse of creative evolution in its relation to the sciences and to the arts, analytic philosophy has chosen instead to focus on the foundations of logic, the problems of natural language, and the purification of all metaphysical categories following Wittgenstein's early mandate: 'the word "philosophy" must mean something which stands above or below, but not beside the natural sciences'.[5] The dominance of the analytic method in most academic departments of philosophy is an effect of the rise of the sciences and technology in the post-war research university and is based on the pretention that the method provides the logical foundations of the sciences themselves. However, this pretention gradually devolved into a 'strongman argument' in philosophy departments across North America especially, and is in some ways based upon the same principle of the strongest difference that one also finds in Schmitt's friend–enemy opposition. The problem is that the strength and the purity of the opposition is almost always decided by the stronger party to the conflict, which has historically resulted in the absence of continental philosophy in many philosophy departments today, except for electives in the history of philosophy. Regarding the question whether or not the division between analytical and continental philosophy is now outdated, it remains a historical dispositif that still determines the academic discipline of philosophy in English-speaking countries, including universities globally that have inherited this disciplinary model either from colonial history or, more recently, through the Anglo-Americanisation of the university system in Eastern Europe, Asia and elsewhere. For example, is not by accident that most continental philosophy is taught in 'the rest of the world' in departments and programmes under the name of 'Cultural Studies', not in Philosophy, nor is it surprising that it is precisely these departments that have recently suffered the most severe cutbacks, and many have been closed or consolidated with the teaching of foreign languages and media studies.

Nevertheless, much of the earlier logical positivism and linguistic-based methods have been abandoned by analytic philosophers themselves in order to update their claim on providing a foundation for the natural sciences, and have been replaced by cognitive and statistical methods that are more conversant with the new methodologies employed in psychology and political science. More recently, philosophy departments in the United States have expanded their faculties to include more specialists on race, gender and sexuality. Thus, the strength of the earlier opposition of continental and analytic has weakened to the point where it could now simply be called two competing 'language games' of philosophy. Of course, according to the players of the analytical game, which is based on a degree of rigour of logic and clarity of expression, the players of the continental language game are often accused of breaking all the rules. Either they are charged with doing 'bad philosophy', or worse, according to the gadfly Brian Leiter, merely creating 'bad literature'. However, when the major difference between two methods (two traditions, or even two 'institutions of modern philosophy') simply comes down to a different way of doing things, or a different way of speaking, then there is no longer a shared concept of identity that could determine which method is the 'best one' (a criteria, by the way, that is supposedly native to the knowledge of both philosophers and butchers since Plato).

In approaching the question 'What is "continental" philosophy?' in its contemporary global context, therefore, I will abandon the identity of difference from an extrinsic, historical, relativistic and/or nationalistic prejudice from which this question usually arises. This is because I do not believe that the continental–analytic opposition gives us any clear and rigorous definition of identity of what is called philosophy today, especially given that many so-called continental philosophers are using more of an analytic style of argumentation (for example, one might think of the style of the thinkers of speculative realism and object-oriented ontology), just as so-called analytic philosophers are being drawn to topics that were formerly located on the continental side of the divide (the emotions, creativity, race, sexual identity, etc.). Most importantly, both traditions have claimed to have abandoned an orthodox position of 'the linguistic turn' that encompassed the leading philosophies of Heidegger *and* Wittgenstein. As a result of all these developments, it is the weakening of opposition between poetry and logic as the twin towers of twentieth-century philosophy that has toppled the board and sent all the pieces flying.

At the same time, if I choose to abandon the previous formulation of 'analytical versus continental' as no longer sufficiently rigorous or clear in conceptualising major difference – that is, if it was anything more than a polemical concept from the very beginning, that is to say, beginning with Russell's attack on Bergson's philosophy in 1922 – I will not abandon altogether the principle of the strongest possible difference in order to pose the question on new ground. In defining the identity of the opposition one must establish the strongest difference of each term, and so I will propose the opposition on the ground of another natural division, which is neither the logical concept, nor following the analogy of an animal's body that is cut up according to its joints. Instead, the difference I will propose to follow is already found to be internal to continental philosophy itself, according to the analogy of the geological fissure, crack or fault line. More specifically, I will employ a geological language to portray an image of thought that can be particularly ascribed to the philosophies of Deleuze and Derrida, since we cannot imagine any history of contemporary continental philosophy that would not be informed by their distinctive concept of difference, which is neither logical nor founded upon a metaphysical principle of reason and, as I will attempt to demonstrate, is inseparable from the manner in which both philosophies have broken away from their natal continent and drifted across the ocean. The question I will take up is how the specific difference that informs the image of geophilosophy can also be derived from the identity of a continental island as opposed to the autochthonous or natal ground of an oceanic island. From Deleuze's earliest writings on this image of thought, we are already presented with a prefiguration of the continental island. As I will return to later, this image directly influences Deleuze's thoughts on the fragmentary nature of the American people in Melville or in Whitman. It is the subject born of a new temporality that cannot be thought without attaching it directly to the Earth, where, as Deleuze says, 'geography and imagination would be one' (DI: 11).

What is a 'continental island'? On an etymological level: 'continent' (from Latin *continere*, to hold together, to connect the parts into a whole) refers precisely to a continuous body of land bordered by water or, differently, to a continuous thought that shapes one's identity and establishes clear borders between it and its surroundings (the desert, the ocean, the other continents, etc.). According to the earlier definition, in the 1953 essay, 'Desert Islands', continental islands are 'born of disarticulation, erosion, fracture; they survive the absorption of what once contained them' (DI: 9). To say that such islands are separated from their former continents in the way that the temporal subject is separated from spatial exteriority is also to restate the event of temporal dislocation and the presence of a lost or absent origin. *Once upon a time* there was an island to which the subject belonged, that is, before the original island (or the earth) vanished in the mist. Consequently, this introduces in the subject's relation to the Earth a feeling of nostalgia and homesickness, or produces an idea of the island that is purely abstract and a-temporal, like Greece. A third possibility will be represented by the continental islands like America and Australia in my analysis, that is, islands that are born from 'disarticulation, erosion, fracture' – one could also say 'migration, loss of origin, ancestral or aboriginal identity' – but which causes both continents to undergo a violent fracture or splitting between an autochthonous and future (or 'destined') Earth. In this sense, the continental island is actually two islands in one land: the desert island (occupied by a native or aboriginal people) and the island of escape or discovery from divine or natural providence, that is, the image created by castaways and so-called 'newcomers'.

By contrast, both England and Germany are originally what Deleuze will define as 'oceanic islands', especially since Germany is an oceanic island that rises up in the middle of the continent of Europe – thus, its autochthonous identification with Greece in Winkelmann and Hölderlin – and because England is an island that has forgotten that it is an island. This can be illustrated both by recent geopolitical movements like Brexit, as well as by England's colonial and oceanic history. The fact 'that England is populated will always come to us as a surprise', as Deleuze says, 'since humans can live on an island only by forgetting what the island represents' (DI: 9). Nevertheless, we should also recall that England was originally a continental island (born by disarticulation and fracture and the erosion strikingly portrayed on the white cliffs of Dover), but the island had gradually drifted across the Channel and distant enough from the continent of Europe that the English themselves eventually forget their own identity as continental subjects, and the island suddenly acquired the sense of a native and original place, or oceanic island. In other words, like Greece, the crown of England suddenly emerged from the ocean, born from the ancient and immemorial strife between the earth and sea. It was in this immemorial time that the earth suddenly erupted and rose vertically to height of the Scafell Pike, and violently pushed back the water into the Channel, on the Southern slope, the North Sea, to the East, and the Irish and Celtic Seas to the West; although, these waters were eventually submerged by the expansion of the island, which grew to border the Atlantic Ocean and the Americas.

Since the main principle of what is called 'geophilosophy' is that, in their ground, 'geography and imagination are one', which the above picture vividly demonstrates, it is the very nature of this strife or violent combat between the land and the sea that grounds the difference between the continental island and the oceanic island, and it is the image of this difference that I will now take up to apply it *philosophically*.

1. The underlying difference – one might even say 'pre-ontological difference' – between the two islands is founded by an extreme opposition, and it is the nature of this opposition that actualises 'the difference of difference', so to speak. In the case of continental islands, the oceans cover the entire surface of the Earth; however, the struggle is located at the periphery, at the edges of the land that undergo erosion and fracture. In the case of oceanic islands, on the other hand, the

land always remains beneath the ocean; thus, the struggle is always located at the centre rather than the periphery, in the volcanic eruption that violently pierces the surface of the ocean in order to establish the ground upon which an habitable earth comes to be erected. It is around this difference between a submerged and violent centre and torn and fragmented periphery that can witness two forms of an an-archic and primordial opposition (*polemos*) that will serve to distinguish the identity of difference philosophically, which is to say, a difference in the nature of the movement that determines the ground of reason.

2. Secondly, let us now turn to an early statement from the essay by Deleuze: 'that an island is deserted must appear *philosophically* normal to us' (DI: 9). Why philosophically, which is italicised here, as if to underline the source of an idea that is neither religious in origin, nor simply belonging to geographical time before humankind? Of course, we know that islands are born before there are humans who come to populate them, that is, before they are territorialised by humankind as well as by different species animals and plants. In other words, there is always an original perspective that belongs to the island itself – namely, *that it is deserted!* It is this original perspective that relates to a primordial difference that must be 'pacified', in every sense of this term, which is to say humanised along with the image of a nature that becomes providential or teleological as a result. Recalling the earlier observation, according to Deleuze, this is because 'humans cannot live, nor live in security, unless they assume that the active struggle between earth and water is now over, or at least contained' (DI: 9). Thus, there is always an 'other island' that pertains to this primordial, active and often violent struggle between the sea and the land (or between *phusis* and *nomos*); therefore, like the English, very early on, or perhaps like present-day Californians, human beings can live on an island by forgetting this 'other island' that is still in movement and continues to tremble under their feet.

3. Third, and finally, it is this geophilosophical articulation of the difference between these two islands, oceanic and continental, both of which are originally deserted and only gradually populated, which also serves as a natural distinction between two kinds of populations or peoples. There are peoples who are originals, that is, who claim to have originally created a unique and indivisible Earth out of their own island; on the other hand, there are peoples whose sense of an

original earth is either derived or mixed with the memories of other islands, who do not claim the earth is their own creation, or that their daily struggle is not in any way unique to them and thus can become a common struggle shared with other peoples and races. For example, one could evoke what Deleuze and Guattari call, following Kafka, the patchwork and fragmentary character of 'minor' or 'small peoples'.

For the purposes of illustration, let us first take up the so-called 'Australian people' who are, as I will demonstrate, distinct from the 'American people'. In both cases, however, there is a third distinction between an aboriginal people and a derived or bastard race in which the meaning of the violent struggle that determines the nature of the continental island is to be located. In fact, the island itself was formed by the struggle of the 'new earth' to push back against the sea, as well as by the trans-generational process of migration, separation, and the deterritorialisation from the memory of other islands, or more primary earths. For example, in the case of the formation of so-called 'Australians' and the 'Americans', both are populations who all originally arrived from the ocean – by various means, according to a number of circumstances, either self-willed and coerced – but then eventually internalised the movement of violent struggle, conflict, and even catastrophe that originally landed them there. This has resulted in a long process of migratory amnesia and a transgenerational traumatised memory that had to be repressed for the sake of survival. For example, neither most Americans nor the majority of Australians remember when they started speaking English, rather than Dutch. Was it their native tongue, the patois of their 'forefathers', or a forced language? Nevertheless, as a result of this long process of migratory amnesia, there also emerged for the majority of these lost and displaced populations a fervent need to lay claim to the island as if it were a promised land, whether we call this new earth 'New Wales' or 'New York', or 'New Amsterdam'. Thus, the original despair of belonging to a bastard race, a race of castaways, the sorry members of a shipwrecked crew, a miserable horde of refugees and survivors, was gradually replaced by a kind of collective 'memory-work', yielding a newfound confidence (a bit presumptuous and unfounded, nonetheless) that both these 'peoples' had in fact landed on firm ground.

As for the so-called 'Australians', however, the cost of occupying a beach head along the Gold Coast up to Melbourne, in order to contain the shark-infested waters that to this day are always nipping at their heels, was a violent effort to push the original desert further into the centre of the continent. Therefore, if Australia can no longer be called a continental island, but has gradually become an oceanic island, like England, it is because it contains the desert as its centre (or origin) since the characteristic of an island is to push the desert to its periphery. In *Perpetual Peace*, Kant argued that the sea is also a desert and there is a strict equivalence between the camel and the ship as seagoing vessels.[6] The desert still remains an 'eternal and sacred place'; thus, the deserted centre distinguishes Australia from other continental islands in that the violent opposition between land and sea is forced to the interior, where one can supposedly find the aboriginal peoples who were displaced by the settlers.

If, today, the 'Australians' have mostly forgotten the violent nature of the original opposition between the subterranean earth and the ocean, or at least believe they have spatially and historically contained it, it was only by forgetting this 'other island' that continues to grow from the middle of their own created wasteland. As an aside, we might see that the contemporary perspective of the Anthropocene was absolutely not an invention of modern palaeontology, but rather the invention of aboriginal peoples who bear the memory of the 'other island' as both a weapon to be employed against the settler race, as well as a much more sophisticated knowledge of the earth than Western sciences have managed to create. As a result, the Australian settler populations (including Chinese and Indonesian newcomers) cling to the coasts like refugees around the sides of a lifeboat in a constant struggle with the desert that threatens to push them back into the ocean, especially given the knowledge that they had all arrived on this island like ballast that had drifted onto the shore after being thrown off their own islands, and by a callous crew who were only attempting the lighten the load a bit.

In the case of the so-called 'American people', although there was a similar process of deterritorialisation of the original continental island, it is not the oceanic island of Defoe's Robinson Crusoe who prefigures the arrival of the English colonisers. Rather, as Deleuze discerned, it is Herman Melville who provides us with a more accurate image of violent nature that represents the birth of the American nation. For example, in *Moby Dick*, the desert-ocean is shown to cover the entire horizon of the earth, and the crew represents all the fragments of humankind who become the motley crew of the *Pequod*, all the bastard classes and races that are cast away together on the same ship and thus have been faced with the task of forming a unity out of this patchwork. And yet, Melville also provides an image of the future in the hulking and mobile form of Moby Dick, the image of a more primordial oceanic island that seems to have become unmoored from its own continent and now wanders the surface of the world's oceans, with its volcanic spout that suddenly punches through the surface of the ocean and constantly threatens to drown, not only the hapless crew of misfits, but the rest of humanity.

It is this struggle with an 'other island' represented by the mobile profile of Moby Dick, or the 'White Whale', that the fatal predicament of an American race is told. Moreover, Ahab's sworn revenge against the whale is the spirit of monomaniacal hatred against a 'Primary Nature' that can serve as the spark of energy to unite all the fragments into the 'great white race'. As Melville shows, the energy or power of this oath consecrating the sovereign right to kill is not a natural right, but a modern industrial power like an electric current that magnetically unites the filaments of lead into one fiery lance, an allegory of the crew of the *Pequod* united by touching the phallic rod of Ahab and swearing an oath of hatred and revenge against a Primary Nature that knows no boundary or natural law. According to Deleuze's reading, it is Ahab's identification with this primary nature that constitutes a war without law, since one can only defeat the Primary Nature enemy by giving oneself over to a war with nature without or beyond all positive law, which in some ways already prefigures the twentieth-century principle of nuclear war.

In the preface to Melville's story 'Bartleby, the Scrivener', written thirty years after the earlier essay we have been discussing, Deleuze will return once more to the theme of the continental versus oceanic island, which is now defined as the modern transformation of the primordial conflict between land and water that is now figured in this 'terrible supersensory Nature, original and oceanic, that knows no law', which pursues its own rationale through the monomaniacal and megalomaniac figures that appear in Melville's fiction almost like hurricanes – that is, Ahab, Claggart, Babo (CC: 79). In his reading, Deleuze refers to what he calls the 'mysterious theory of two natures' (CC: 80–1), one which is primary and original, and the other which is secondary and sensible, and which is governed by laws. It is this same conflict between two natures that we addressed above as the primordial conflict between earth and water that humankind must either forget altogether, or, at least, believe that its chaos has been pacified in order to rescue a chance of peace and security in living with the 'Primary Nature'. Deleuze's implicit comparison of this 'terrible supersensory Nature' to so-called natural disasters is neither accidental nor arbitrary. In fact, a tsunami or hurricane represents a Primary Nature that suddenly punches through the rational order of the Secondary Nature imposed by human knowledge and thus testifies to a more powerful nature that knows nothing of this secondary order. Thus, the creation of technology and the modern sciences, which have replaced religion and superstition as a rationalising factor (or what Bergson identified as the principle of falsification and myth-making) can only pretend to give a secondary and completely ineffective order to this Primary Nature, that is, an image of the law that belongs only to the secondary and sensible nature created by human beings. However, a tsunami or hurricane does not follow any idea of law, even physical laws (which are simply metaphorical), in determining the path it will take as it approaches the coastline, but seems to exhibit a menacing and arbitrary will to violate every law of physics in suddenly changing direction to wreak havoc on the most densely populated areas. What is unique to Melville's symbolism is the internalisation of a Primary Nature in a sovereign being like Ahab, who appears like a modern Moses, but along with the psychological motives of hatred and revenge as a causal explanation of violence and death, beyond any human law, that becomes the principal attribute of this Primary Nature.

In some ways, the novels of Defoe and Melville both reveal a primordial rift between the first two natures, which occurs at some point in the beginning in the nineteenth century along with the decline of the myth-making power of religion to pacify the fear of the Primary Nature, and rise of the belief in modern technology and industrial capitalism as the principle of a third nature that will enter in to do battle and overpower it. As if already anticipating Derrida's commentary in the lectures on *The Beast and the Sovereign*, Deleuze already interprets Defoe's novel philosophically as the source of a new mythology that supplants the powers of religion as the fabulating faculty for creating both the gods and the world. Deleuze writes: 'Literature is an attempt to interpret, in an ingenious way, the myths we no longer understand, at the very moment we no longer reproduce them.' In other words, Defoe's novel becomes emblematic of a modern myth in the form that is no longer represented as myth, because it represents the death of a previous form of myth and the birth of a new form of myth that will replace it: the myth of everyday bourgeois life that all the more powerful because it appears on an oceanic island, in absolute solitude, where Robinson establishes his 'natural order' simply by reconstructing, translating the daily and petty rituals of the new bourgeois order. In some ways, however, this also limits the universality of *Robinson Crusoe* as a representation of modern myth, since it is also a psychological novel and culturally bound as an English comedy of manners. Both Virginia Woolf and Michel Tournier later satirised the bourgeois order of the island: for Woolf, it is typically an English desire to prefer a slave to a member of the other sex. Recalling Deleuze's commentary on the 'Robinson myth' in Michel Tournier's brilliant palimpsest, *Vendredi*, Deleuze employs the novel as a philosophical allegory in order to 'deconstruct' the bourgeois myth of the Secondary Nature and the revelation of 'another Island' (LS: 301–21). For example, Tournier describes Robinson's fastidious 'house economy' in meticulous detail, since the English dream of a world that is ordered like a wardrobe of immaculate linens scented with lavender.

I have used Derrida's term 'deconstruction' in the above description intentionally to render the proximity of Deleuze's interpretation of the secondary nature of culture as the 'supplement' of an Original or Primary Nature in *Of Grammatology*, which appears the same year as the *Logic of Sense* (1969). It is precisely at this point, or peninsula, that the two major philosophies of difference meet together 'on continental grounds', so to speak, that is, before Derrida leaves for America and Deleuze chooses to remain in Paris and take a more schizophrenic voyage. For example, as Deleuze writes, 'First, it is true that from the deserted island it is not creation but re-creation, not the beginning but the re-beginning that takes place.' Thus, the very power of the model is not in its production, but its repetition; 'the second origin is thus more essential than the first, since it gives us the law of repetition, the law of the series, whose first origin gave us only moments' (DI: 13). As for Derrida's philosophy of difference, I would ask whether the movement of deconstruction itself can be understood as an expression of a continental drift – that is, caused by disarticulation, fracture, and the erosion of the original model by the power of the copy, a copy which is actually revealed to be more primary than the original. In some manner, the style of deconstruction is thoroughly continental, that is to say, a style of difference that recapitulates the migratory movement of leaving one's own island, supplanting the primordial origin of the oceanic island with a new archipelago of continental islands.

To demonstrate that is association is not merely metaphorical, I will refer to well-known passages from *Of Grammatology*, where Derrida first returns to the 'Nature Philosophy' of Rousseau, which he also later calls a 'Robinsonade'.[7] Moreover, it is not by accident that this is where he first introduces the term – not really a concept – of 'a dangerous supplement', and where he first demonstrates the procedure that the term represents by taking up the nature/culture, original/supplement, primary/secondary distinction.[8] Again, we remember that the continent names a process borne of disarticulation, separation, fracture; the separation between original and secondary nature. Thus, the continental subject qua subject is one who experiences this process of separation, disarticulation, fracture, and survives it in a certain manner by 'living on' (*continuer*), not by erasing the presence of the original island, since the continental island is not revealed as a new island, but rather a fragment of the original, even an 'exterior addition' (which is also the definition of the 'supplement' in *Le Petit Robert*).

In this manner, writing is a supplement to speech, culture is a supplement to nature, the sign is the supplement to the thing itself; however, these distinctions only appear and even only make sense from the subjective experience of a continental process of diffraction and separation. In other words, it would make no sense from the perspective of an oceanic island, as in the case of Rousseau, who could only express the negativity that marks the loss of an original island, caused by the lack that culture (specifically agriculture) introduces into nature, the lack from which also emerges the desire to return to the original island in order to recreate from pure memory what had been carelessly lost: first speech, then nature, and finally, the Thing itself.

This is an itinerary that Derrida will also track down in Heidegger's path when he points out how the question of the world, the animal and the stone is proposed *as if from the perspective of someone living on a desert island!* Consequently, following this series to their ground, Derrida returns to the question of 'world' by first asking the question: 'What is an island?'

> Why does one love islands? Why does one not love islands? Why do some people love islands while others do not love islands, some people dreaming of them, seeking them out, inhabiting them, taking refuge on them, and others avoiding them, even fleeing them instead of taking refuge on them? But fleeing them, as much as taking refuge on them, presupposes a movement of flight. One cannot dissociate the figure of the island from the experience

of flight. For example, one can long for the island as for a distant refuge to which one could flee humanity for a chosen exile.[9]

The itinerary spelled out in Derrida's earliest attempt to deconstruct what he called 'Western ethno-centric reason' finds its destination in the deconstruction of the concept of world in Heidegger in the second lecture course of *The Beast and the Sovereign*. In fact, perhaps the entire itinerary can be understood, *philosophically*, as the deconstruction of the philosophical genre of the oceanic island. For example, here I would underline the dominant characteristic in Derrida's reading together the figure of sovereign exception and the philosophical novel of *Robinson Crusoe*; both figures emerge out of an exceptional solitude and a state of exception from which the world is also created. At the same time, there is the revelation of an unbridgeable distance between two worlds. In Derrida's words:

> [T]he difference between one world and another will remain always unbridgeable, because the community of the world is always constructed, simulated by a set of stabilizing apparatuses, more or less stable, then, and never natural, language in the broad sense, codes of traces being designed, among all living beings, to construct a unity of the world that is always deconstructible, nowhere and never given in nature. . . . Between my world, the 'my world', what I call 'my world' – and there is no other for me, as any other world is part of it – between my world and any other world there is first the space and the time of an infinite difference, an interruption that is incommensurable with all attempts to make a passage, a bridge, an isthmus, all attempts at communication, translation, trope, and transfer that the desire for a world or the want of a world, the being wanting a world will try to pose, impose, propose, stabilize. There is no world, there are only islands. That is one of the thousand directions in which I would be < tempted > to interpret the last line of a short and great poem by Celan: '*Die Welt ist fort, ich muss dich tragen*', a poem of mourning or birth that I do not have time to read with you: the world has gone, the world has gone away, the world is far off, the world is lost, there is no world any more.[10]

In response, at this point I would simply ask whether it is possible, without changing the semantic meaning of both terms too much, meta-phorically to substitute the Heideggerian concept of world with the term 'island' or 'oceanic island'? Thus, *the island has gone, the island has gone away, the island is too far off, the island is lost, there is no island anymore.* Maintaining this lexical substitution of 'an island' for 'a world' clearly in view (a substitution not only of concepts or *philosophemes*, but one of territory and orientation), let us now return to Heidegger, whom earlier I had identified as an oceanic philosopher, whom Derrida will also refer to as 'Heidegger-Robinson'.[11] Instead of continuing our reading of the second lecture course of *The Beast and the Sovereign*, however, instead I will turn to the very late post-war seminar *Was heist Denken?* where Heidegger himself covertly returns to the Robinsonian theme of the desert island in meditating on the refrain from Nietzsche: 'the wasteland grows from within'.[12] At this point, in the immediate post-war period of 1951–2, the lonely German philosopher returns to some of the same themes of the earlier Rectorate Address by describing the German *Volk* as being literally 'caught in the pincers' of the two great mass societies of the United States and the Soviet Union. Moreover, Germany is also threatened by the loss of its autochthonous identification with Greece, which was the anchor of New Humanism under Wolf, Paulsen, Lessing, Humboldt and, of course, Hölderlin. Perhaps echoing the later refrain, 'the people are missing', it is the disappearance of the aboriginal German–Greek identity that now threatens to completely eclipse the recovery of an authentic German *Volk*, especially after the catastrophe brought about by Hitler who betrays the people and shipwrecks the destiny of the German nation.

It is precisely in this situation that we can now picture Heidegger as a castaway and solitary thinker on his own 'island of despair'. 'The wasteland grows' (*Die Wüste wächst*), our shipwrecked castaway complains, echoing the earlier phrase from Zarathustra, the convalescent. In other words, 'there is no more world', which I have translated above as 'no more oceanic island'. Although the translator chooses the term 'wasteland', perhaps giving it a more apocalyptic tone, *Wüste* should more accurately rendered according to our island metaphors: 'The desert grows! Woe to him who hides the desert within!' In his own reading of this passage, it is not by chance that Derrida hears the echo of the original pessimism and world-weariness of a certain Jean-Jacques Rousseau. With this refrain, Heidegger speaks of an interior desert that now grows in the centre of Europe, in the voice of Zarathustra, but who also proposes himself as the last philosopher in the West, but only because, after Nietzsche, he is the first thinker to actually hear (which means 'to heed, to obey') the prophetic statement from Nietzsche's own philosophy that 'the most thought-provoking thought in our thought-provoking time is that we are not yet thinking'.[13]

The wasteland, and the growing of the wasteland (i.e., the desert, and the growing of the desert), is joined together with Nietzsche's words to prophesy a future to which the entire earth is destined to its remotest corners.[14] Are these not words that could only be spoken on a desert island, that is, by someone who was thrown there (*geworfen*), who finds himself a castaway, and whose feelings of despair were so intensively and existentially felt that this subjective interiority grows outwards and threatens to cast its shadow to the remotest corners of the earth? Thus, the world is gone, and this island, this island of loneliness and despair, is everywhere! Moreover, with all this talk of destiny, destination and being destined, also now hear an uncanny resonance with another voice, which is Heidegger's own, before the war, concerning the coming of a 'fateful decision' for the German *Volk*, which we know has become a shadow that at this point covers his entire philosophy. Therefore, we must now hear this shadow speak as well, even though it mostly remains silent and actually speaks nowhere in the 1951 lecture course. Or does it? In order to hear this shadow, allow me to render it in Heidegger's own voice: 'What did the Second World War really decide?' (*Was hat der zweite Weltkrieg eigentlich entshieden?*). Heidegger suddenly poses this fateful question, and then immediately adds the following: 'We shall not mention here its fearful consequences for my country [*unser Vaterland*], cut in two [*zu schweigen*])'.[15] The translator chooses to place this statement in parenthesis, which it is not in the original German text, as if it remained unspoken, perhaps like an interior monologue that should not be heard on the same level as the question. Here, I would merely underline, now in a Derridean voice, it is this statement in parenthesis that speaks of something left unsaid, even as something that is 'unmentionable', precisely concerning Heidegger's own feelings regarding consequences of the war on '*unser Vaterland*'. These are the words of the prophet speaking from his desert island, concerning 'our future', but they could just as easily have been the words of Rousseau speaking of Europe immediately after the earthquake in Lisbon, or the contemporary philosopher in view of the pandemic.

Turning now to read the half-spoken statement itself, in referring to his country being cut in two, once again this echoes the statement that described his country, immediately before the war, as being caught in the pincers between two great superpowers. So the war has now cut his country in half, and yet, as he immediately goes on to say, it has actually 'decided' nothing (*Dieser Weltkrieg hat nichts entscheiden*)[16] – 'if we here to use "decision" in so high and wide a manner that it concerns solely man's essential fate on this earth'.[17] As if to add insult to injury, the complainant continues, the scissors of the Enlightenment has only made 'a patchwork of the earth'.[18] Modern democracy is nothing but patchwork and is still in decline, perhaps even more so after the war. The desert grows. It is now growing in the middle of the European continent. 'Even in the decade from 1920 to 1930', he reflects on the pre-war period, before the rise of National Socialism, the European world of ideas could not cope any longer with what was looming on the horizon. What is to become now of a Europe that wants to rebuild itself with the stage props of those years after the First World War? His answer: 'A plaything for the powers, and for the immense native strength [*Volkskraft*] of the Eastern peoples'.[19] Of course, this was already Nietzsche's prophecy concerning the world of European ideas (democracy and a European Union, or *foidus pacificum*), as set forth in the *Twilight of the Idols* in 1888 (i.e., 'Democracy has always been a form of decline in organising power') and ten years earlier in *Human, All Too Human* in 1878, where he writes concerning the native instincts of the Russian people as a 'counter-concept to the miserable European particularism'. Heidegger updates and redacts Nietzsche's nineteenth-century prophecy: 'Nietzsche's concern is to think beyond the teeming multitude of nationalisms which, as even he saw then, are no longer viable, and to clear the field for the great decisions – for reflection on these decisions'.[20] Once again, I underline this word: *decision*, 'in its highest and widest sense of the term'. In fact, this word itself returns *ad nauseam* throughout this seminar of 1951, before Heidegger loses his voice (the prophetic voice of Nietzsche) and turns back to Aristotle to reflect on the most essential and 'fateful decision that perhaps as been made in the West', a decision that lies at the very origin of everything that will come after it: the Aristotelian decision of man as an *animal rationale* as that 'rising presence which can make appear what is present'. But even this decision has been muddled by the time of the Romans, in order to become a peculiar combination of animality and rationality, body and soul, human and animal, reason and instinctual power, and so forth. Nevertheless, it is precisely at this moment in the lecture that Heidegger declares that he no longer hears this prophetic word today, in the contemporary moment, and in the later part of this last seminar recommends to his students that they read instead Aristotle for fifteen years. In other words, perhaps *it is too late for us moderns or contemporaries*, too late for any essential reflection on this fateful decision of the Greeks, which, owing to the lack of attention of the Roman thinkers, first, and then the fateful inattention and forgetfulness of the Christian and Enlightenment thinkers that followed, has turned the island of Europe into a desert that now grows within every individual subject and every people, creating a *patchwork of particularisms.*

It is necessary to hear the above statements as 'symptomatic' in the Nietzschean sense, that is, as the words of a 'convalescent' (which I discussed earlier). Or they are 'signals' of an affective mood, according to Heidegger's own existential analytic of *Dasein's* fundamental attunement to moribundity, as 'being thrown toward death and despair'. Or, finally, they are simply the direct expressions of Heidegger's own moribund feelings immediately after the war – feelings of desolation, self-pity (a kind of 'woe is me'), coupled with feelings of home sickness, nostalgia, the memories of the other shore, of the 'other island'. After all, is not Heidegger the moodiest of all modern philosophers? Is this not the implicit reason for Derrida's forced coupling of these two figures (Heidegger–Robinson) to reveal more strongly the effects of homesickness and nostalgia, as well as the coming decision concerning the new and more barbarous *animal rationale* that Heidegger sees on the horizon, in reflecting on the most fateful decision of the rational animal from a historical context where – it has already been declared by the voice from out of the desert – '*nothing has been decided*'. In the end, the world war, the Holocaust, the supposed triumph of Western democratic states, amount to nothing at all in the face of the most ancient and most fateful 'decision' concerning the *animal rationale.*

At this point, I will conclude my reflections on the European oceanic island by referring the reader once again to Derrida's acute interrogation of Heidegger's 'Robinsonade'. In order to begin philosophising from original questions such as 'What is world?', 'What is man?', 'What is an animal?' or 'What is finitude?' From now on, one must begin with the presupposition that today one finds oneself alone on a desert island. And yet, we have discovered that there are no more desert islands today. That is to say, in the current stage of globalisation – whether it is 'early', or 'advanced', still remains undecided, although I think we can certainly agree it is not yet 'late'! – there are no more oceanic islands. Consequently, it would naturally follow from this conclusion that *there can be no more oceanic philosophies from now on! No more desert islands, ergo, no more Robinsonades!* Concerning the figure of the desert, or what Derrida calls in 'Faith and Knowledge' the 'desert in the desert',[21] referring to the translation of the Platonic *khora*, we would need to carefully reconstruct this semantic and conceptual figure of a desert from which neither religious prophecy nor philosophical sovereignty emerges, but which is the name for a place that does not let itself be dominated by any theological, ontological revelation, that is more ancient than any opposition, including perhaps the opposition of original versus derived or supplemental, cultural or historical upon which Heidegger's image of reason is always premised upon the recovery of a more original ground. Although there is not time to reflect on what Derrida might mean by 'the desert in the desert', I would simply point to this *topos* or place without image as something that emerges against any claim to be original, even though it is said to be 'more ancient' than any opposition than any ground, even more ancient than the distinction between religion, philosophy and sovereign law. Moreover, in the contemporary age, even the attempt to create a desert island philosophy would be morally suspect, since one can no longer begin philosophising from a position of innocence and forgetting. And what I mean by this is that one cannot begin philosophising as if on a deserted island asking the questions of the kind 'What is a man? an animal? a stone? an object? a god? a world?' and so on. If there are no more desert islands, one can no longer begin asking questions 'as if' (*als ob*) we lived on an oceanic island, or that one could return to own's own island. *In other words, there is no longer any 'original question' in philosophy. Instead, from here on there is only the question of difference and of repetition.*

Does this imply that now there are only continental islands, as if from now on, there is only continental philosophy 'born of disarticulation, fracture, etc.'? Yes and no. I would say 'yes' from the perspective of the current world picture in which all our islands are connected by the global world market and there are no longer desert islands which would provide the position of 'remoteness' necessary for the affective mood of *theoria*, as has been argued lately by new materialists and feminists alike, and certainly no distant vantage point or 'bird's-eye view' necessary for the construction of a transcendental point of view. In short, there is no privileged position, nor is there any remaining privilege for one's own island as the ground upon which the world can be constructed. Today, instead, every world is implicated in every other world, animal, plant, human, cybernetic – we are all implicated in this world. Even the Aristotelian construction of the *animal rationale* is only the flotsam that appears like foam in the tide, or rather, the jetsam that washes up on the shore having been tossed overboard to lighten the vessel of being. This is the reason, in my last book, I privilege Kant's idea of universal cosmo-politanism, because it opposes any oceanic philosophy. In *Perpetual Peace*, there can only be continental islands, because of the *universal commercium* (as one might say today, the global market). The only oceanic islands that remain are still the nation states, which in the eighteenth century Kant compared to rogues and brigands on the desert-ocean, and who are still very much acting the rogue today, as sovereigns who can only wage war as the condition of their right to exist.

And yet, if we were to judge the world picture of continental islands by the map that has been provided by a certain historical and geograph-ical tradition of continental philosophy just over the past ninety years or so, then I would also say 'no', simply because the map of the conti-nents looks more like a child's drawing or one of those pictures of the globe from the Middle Ages. According to this child's drawing, Europe would encompass an enlarged centre (no longer the minor cap of Asia), Africa would form an island along the southern coast, Australia would be an eastern peninsula (perhaps replacing Korea). South America and Mexico would not exist as known territories; and all the islands of the Pacific remain to be discovered. China and India for the most part would still be reduced to one of those charming fables that appear in the *Ficciones* of Borges. As for America and England? The island of Locke and Berkeley would certainly be represented, but probably floating in the middle of the Atlantic, halfway to the United States, which itself is a continental island torn from Ireland and consisting mostly of an archi-pelago of city-islands – New York, Baltimore, Philadelphia, Chicago – and then, westward, the vast inner sea of desert of the Midwest, until you land in Los Angeles and San Francisco. (In fact, on the map of continental philosophy, the map of the United States would resemble Australia in most respects.)

It is clear from the description above that my definition of continental philosophy refers to no existing tradition or institution of contemporary philosophy, but rather to a future image of thought that will only be born of further disarticulation, fracture, erosion of the earlier dichoto-mies and disciplinary traditions, and so on. As for analytic philosophy? In the same manner perhaps that the future discipline of continental philosophy will no longer simply be a reflection of one continental drift (the postcolonial drifting of the European continent), following a similar pattern of 'disarticulation', the more the method departs from a formal and axiomatised logic by incorporating the developments of modern neuroscience in the picture of the mind, or the study of rational and cognitive systems, it will no longer be possible to oppose its formal method or logic to that of another branch or style of philosophy, especially since continental philosophers are also turning to the sciences of biology, physics and neuroscience as well. On this point I am only speculating, but I believe that much in the same way that the old binaries (such as East/West, male/female, nature/culture) that were originally derived from a linguistic system of differences have been deconstructed and multiplied through a process that resembles the geological movement of disarticulation, erosion and fracturing that results in an archipelago of continental islands, the old dichotomy of analytic versus continental will someday erode completely, just as every oceanic island will one day ultimately sink beneath the rising tide of the world's oceans. Like the philosophy of Greece, the origin will exist only as the ancient myth of the Earth as in Hesiod.

Notes

1. Gutting, 'Bridging the Continental Divide'.
2. Wittgenstein *Culture and Value*, p. 21.
3. Bergson, *The Creative Mind*, pp. 60ff.
4. Bergson, An Introduction to Metaphysics, p. 1.
5. Wittgenstein, Tractatus Logico-Philosophicus 4.111.
6. Kant, Perpetual Peace and Other Essays, 118.
7. Derrida, *The Beast and the Sovereign*, vol. 2, p. 33.
8. Derrida, *Of Grammatology*, 141–57.
9. Derrida, *The Beast and the Sovereign*, vol. 2, p. 64.
10. Ibid., p. 9.
11. Ibid., p. 31.
12. Heidegger, *What is Called Thinking?*, pp. 64ff.
13. Ibid., p. 6.
14. Ibid., p. 65.
15. Ibid.
16. Ibid.
17. Ibid., p. 66.
18. Ibid.
19. Ibid., p. 65.
20. Ibid., p. 68.
21. Derrida, 'Faith and Knowledge', pp. 58ff.

3. The Archipelago of Contemporary Reason

'. . . trouver, sinon ce qui peut légitimer le jugement (le "bon"
enchaînement), du moins comment sauver l'honneur de penser.'

Lyotard, *Le Différend*

The Three Archipelagos of Political Reason

If we were to conceive of an image of thought in which 'geography
and imagination are one' (Deleuze), we might find an initial sketch of
this image in Jean-François Lyotard's late philosophy where we find an
archipelago of continental islands. Consequently, if I said previously that
one cannot imagine any contemporary image of thought that has not
been informed by the two major philosophies of difference (namely, the
philosophies of Deleuze and Derrida); however, it is the philosophy of *le
différend* that offers the most literal translation of the concept of difference
into the language of geophilosophy.

Much of Lyotard's effort in the last works is to create what he calls
passages or crossings (*Übergängen*) between the three senses of the archipelago that are 'dispersed' throughout Kant's late political writings.
Whatever the *cause* of this dispersion is a subject of intense speculation,
but may simply come down to the fact that Kant died before being able
to compose the metaphysical elements of politics (*le politique*) in the same
manner as the first three critiques. Of course, others have argued that
such a metaphysics would never have been possible to begin with and
that Kant would have been mad to conceive of its possibility; or that he
was senile at the end of his life. Regardless, whatever the *cause*, following Lyotard's major claim, the 'Critique of Political Reason was never
written' (E: 11), and yet the proper field or 'object' of such a potential
critique can indeed be found dispersed in a number of discrete 'signs'

that appear like a chain of islands in an archipelago, and according to the three following senses:

1. *First Sense*: The dispersion of Kant's late writings on politics do not form a systematic critique of political reason, but nevertheless may constitute a preliminary map of the isolines of this future critique, and thus I emphasise it is a critique that remains to be fashioned and I would describe Lyotard's attempt as providing only a 'sketch' (*Entwurf*), also a preliminary draft of a critique of political reason. Therefore, it seems completely appropriate for me to enter into this draft to continue to revise or refine it, so we must first of all not treat Lyotard's draft as a final work, or, in short, a political philosophy.

2. *Second Sense*: The dispersion of the faculties is exemplarily 'dramatised' already in Kant in the determination of the sublime presentation (*Darstellung*), which can no longer be regulated or legislated by the understanding in the speculative interest of reason. In this example, the 'faculty' of judgement – if it is indeed a 'faculty' or a 'power', and Lyotard will always question this nomination – is called upon to supply a passage (a determinate concept) between intuition and experience and utterly fails to unify the presentation, causing the faculties themselves to enter into an heterogenous and 'discordant' relation to one another, once again, in the manner of an archipelago of the faculties. Lyotard only further dramatises or exaggerates the situation of this heterogeneity of the original Kantian faculties by defining them as phrase families, following Wittgenstein's critical conception of judgement, which Lyotard claims that he derives from Kant in order to redefine the faculty of judgement: 'And in my narrative of the history of philosophy', he says, 'this is where the Wittgenstein of the *Philosophical Investigations* directly picks up the relay of critique. That is why I use the expression *phrase family* where Kant says *representation*' (E: 9).

3. Finally, the third sense or image of the archipelago is the dispersion of the idea of human community (an idea of world) into an archipelago of what I have called, following Deleuze, 'continental islands'. As I have suggested earlier on, it in this last dispersion that I will assign the question of Europe today: Europe is a continental island in an archipelago of other islands, such as the Americas, Africa and Asia. This is the contemporary archipelago of political reason, which reveals gaps between different human communities, and even between different

histories that no longer belong to the same past and, consequently, may no longer share the same future. As a result, we are presented with the loss of an 'idea' that represents – even in a regulative, purely virtual or schematic manner – the complete extension of a community of reasonable beings in a world, which was formerly an 'object' of philosophical representation (or 'phrase regimen'). In part, I am taking my definition of the continental island from Deleuze, who said that continental islands are borne of 'disarticulation, erosion, and fracture that survive the absorption of what once contained them' (DI: 9). However, this sense can also be found in Lyotard as well, who often describes the faculty of judgement as an admiral who launches ships from one island to the next to bring back not just empirical data (acquired through war or commerce), but also rules of formation and connection (i.e., 'phrase families and genres of discourse') (D: 130–2)

Concerning the last image of an archipelago composed of continental islands, I realise that I am not employing the geological term precisely, but only to dramatise the dispersion of territories and continents into distinctive formations brought about by the failure of the powers of imagination, reason and understanding – what Kant constituted as the faculties – to conceive of the cosmopolitical constitution of the community of intelligent beings. I could also demonstrate this by tearing up a map of the world and then strewing the torn pieces on the floor, except that, in order to be accurate, I would have to tear up the continuum of time and space itself that is assumed a priori to condition the possibility of a unity expressed in geometrical or mathematical schema, and is the basis for any cartography. There is also a narrative form of temporal presentation of the idea of community that I will address later, since this will play an important role in Kant's last writings on human history. As I already observed, Europe would only be one continental island or human community among others, according to one cultural *Bildungsroman* traditionally associated with the 'Enlightenment', in which the European community has formerly enjoyed the role of the protagonist in this philosophical novel. The question that will occur to us naturally is whether Europe still plays this role today, which is far from certain (even by the fact that one cannot say there is one community, or even a practical or regulative idea of the European Union of Nations), and I would even say more and more placed in question in light of contemporary events, and exposed as a fiction by various political antagonists. I will not enter into the question of who might emerge to assume the role of the protagonist of this novel today.

Although Lyotard will announce the failure of a certain *Bildungsroman* of reason in his earlier and formative definition of the postmodern condition (i.e., the decline of the grand narrative of progress in human history), one could argue that Kant had already foreseen this failure in his late political writings, especially *Towards Perpetual Peace*, when he argued that the complete metaphysical system of justice, the elements of which he laid out in the *Rechtslehre* (1795/1798) could not even be attempted until a list of preliminary conditions have been met that would establish the basis (or ground) for the critical tribunal of reason to practically enter into any discussion of the Cosmo political constitution of humanity, the most important of which is the cessation of wars promulgated by the nation states. As long as even a portion of humanity is under the threat of war, he declares in an important passage, there cannot be any justice for the whole species. At the same time, Kant also outlined many arguments against the success of his own 'sketch' of human history (at which point he must resort to a fable of natural or divine providence), particularly the consolidation of the nation-states premised upon the 'right of war' (*ius bellum*), the continued involvement and expansion of Europe in the colonial project, and the weakening of international law to the point, he declares in a critical prophecy, that humankind will become so disposed against one another that the idea of perpetual peace will become a wide-open grave piled with corpses.

Of course, the reality of this wide-open grave that was bored into the European continent less than two centuries later is named 'Auschwitz', and thus it is not by accident that it appears as the first case concerning of the dispersion of the universal political reason, as well as the beginning of the moment of the 'downgoing' (*Untergangen*) of the European protagonist in the cultural *Bildungsroman* of the history of reason, which is to say the novel we have been reading and rewriting in several different versions for the last century. For lack of time, and because well known, I will not go further into this part of the European novel, except to observe that it is offered as the first explanation of the dispersion of political reason in *The Differend*. Lyotard also argues against the entire tradition of neo-Kantian scholarship by claiming what is often called 'The Doctrine of Right' (*Rechtslehre*) or the Second Critique 'is not the pertinent text for the study of the political in Kant' (E: 9). Whatever the reasons, once again, the 'Critique of Political Reason was never written' (E: 11). Therefore, what originally existed only as a sketch in Kant assumes the form of notes and experimental *Passagenwerk* in Lyotard's late philosophy.

The 'situation' of *Le Différend*

As I have just described, if the 'field' of the critique of political reason is summarily 'dispersed' throughout a number of 'heterogenous phrase families', whose arrangement can best be represented by an archipelago of continental islands, then the 'object' of critique is, according to Lyotard, *le différend* is not a phrase, but rather the feeling that arises from an unstable state and instant of language wherein something calls to be put into phrases, but cannot yet be (D: 13).

First, let us recall that *The Différend* begins with three cases, as if presented before the critical tribunal. The first of which is most commonly associated with the argument, of course, is the testimony of a holocaust victim concerning the reality of the gas chambers, as evidence of the Final Solution, which the opposing party denies for lack of actual eyewitnesses. The differend appears when absolute verification is demanded, which would be immune to the failure of language to establish the rule of judgement between opposing parties. The second case is the judgement of an anonymous masterpiece that was never published, and thus is known only to the author. This is the speculative genre of philosophy and its myth of natural genius (or what Deleuze refers to as the Greek myth of the 'celestial stranger'), but which pathetically depends on historical and disciplinary protocols of legitimation that are not immune to error, and have even exposed the completely redacted text of reason to various catastrophes. How many great works of philosophy have gone completely unrecognised, as if the universe of phrases was engulfed in a grand conspiracy against the truth? 'Can you give me, says the editor defending his or her profession, the title of a work of major importance which would have been rejected by every editor and would therefore remain unknown?' (D: 4). No. There is only silence, or multiple silences, that exist in the void opened at the base or ground of the history of philosophy like the damned in Virgil. In this case, Lyotard shows, the argument takes the same form as in the previous case and establishes the problem of the differend: 'reality' is not given to this or that subject, but rather the state of the referent that results from the effectuation of establishment protocols; accordingly, the publishing industry would be the protocol that governs the second case, just as historical inquiry would govern the first (D: 4).

However, it is the third case offered by Lyotard – the one that most readers have skipped over, or simply stopped reading altogether, since they were satisfied that this work was ultimately about the status of Holocaust testimony – where we might find some implicit commentary on the establishment procedures of certain modern historico-critical tribunals of political reason, including those that operate especially in the North American university today under the protocols of identity politics. It is drawn from the satirical Russian novel *The Yawning Heights* by Alexander Zinoviev, and is formulated in the following paraphrase:

> Either Ibanskian is not a communist, or he is. If he is, he has no need to testify, . . . since he admits that the communist authorities are the only ones competent to effectuate the establishment procedures for the reality of the communist character of that society. If he ceases to give his agreement to these authorities, . . . there is, in this case, no more credit to be accorded to his testimony than to that of a human being who says he communicated with aliens. (D: 4)

In either case, the object of the judgement in question is an idea of historical-political reason (i.e., the communist character, or any social identity as such), which is not an object of cognition, and since there exists no such protocol *in general and universally* for establishing the reality of subjective identity, unless one defers all judgement concerning the reality of the subject to a certain tribunal of political reason, which is totalitarian in principle since any differend over the claim of identity is prohibited as an object of dispute. (I think the analogy to the contemporary establishment protocols for the critical tribunal of identity politics is fairly self-evident in this example.) Implicitly drawing upon the Kantian critique of transcendental illusion, Lyotard claims that a differend occurs anytime the reality of an idea of political reason is established by means of a protocol employed for an object of cognition. 'That's why it is important to distinguish between phrase regimens, and this comes down to limiting the competence of a given tribunal to a given kind of phrase' (D: 4–5).

'In all three cases', Lyotard concludes, 'to the privation constituted by the damage there is added the impossibility of bringing the case to the knowledge of others, and in particular to the knowledge of a tribunal. This is what a wrong (*tort*) would be: a damage (*dommage*) accompanied by the loss of means to prove the damage' (D: 5). In response to this situation, Lyotard invokes a common law protocol as the basis for determining the concept of the differend, that is to say, an area of tort law that exists outside or before the codex of criminal legal codes in which the determination of the wrong in question is based on positive laws (*Gesetz*). In common law jurisprudence, if a similar dispute has been resolved in the past, the court is usually bound to follow the reasoning used in the prior decision (a principle known as *stare decisis*); therefore, it is only a preceding phrase that is 'linked' to the current one, and thereby converting a *damage* into a *wrong*. If, however, the court finds that the current dispute is fundamentally distinct from all previous cases, and legislative statutes are either silent or ambiguous on the question, judges have the authority and duty to resolve the issue (since one party or the other has to win) and can make a decision 'in the case' by a form of judgement called a 'matter of first impression'. Here, we find the principle, if not the temporality, of the specific type of 'judgement' that Lyotard employs in the concept or situation of a differend, which can be distinguished from the Kantian concept of *Recht* (also *ius*, *le droit*), as I will say more about in a moment. Consequently, the objective of Lyotard's reflection on the situation of the differend is precisely to discover those damages that, as of yet, have not been able to be phrased according to any precedent or prior judgement – that is to say, those differends that exist without phrases, and thus cannot establish the reality of their damage. As Lyotard writes, 'it is in the nature of a victim not to be able to prove that one has been done a wrong. A plaintiff is someone who has incurred damages and who disposed of the means to prove it. One becomes a victim if one loses these means' (D: 8).

At this point, let us invoke the situation of a subjective feeling that arises from an unstable state and instant of language wherein something calls to be put into phrases, but yet cannot be (D: 13). One can say, for example, 'I have suffered an injustice', and this is certainly a phrase, but the phrase would fall upon deaf ears unless it was also accorded a protocol for establishing the reality of a wrong. It would amount to no more than saying, 'I have communicated with aliens' or 'I have an unconscious toothache', and would be dismissed as a form of nonsense. As is often the case, lacking any protocol, the phrase would be seen as tantamount to lying, and an accusation of madness would immediately ensue. For example, the tribunal might say: 'What you are calling a damage is really not a wrong. Therefore, you merely imagined it, just as if you imagined speaking with aliens' (D: 13–15). If the plaintiff persists in invoking the reality of a wrong, lacking any legitimation protocols, then she really would be mad, and so the plaintiff usually chooses to fall silent rather than pursue the claim further and risk something much worse than suffering the damage in silence. You see what I am getting at here is a certain historico-political determination of a certain feeling of madness at the basis of the situation of the differend, as demonstrated in all three cases above where there is an experience nonetheless but lacking any means of establishing its reality. The victims of the extermination are all dead. You cannot tell me the title of the unpublished manuscript. Either Ibanskian is not a communist, or else he is. *Period!*

On the basis of the above observations, we can propose the following statement as an axiom: *the silence of the universe of damages is infinitely larger, quantitatively speaking, than a finite number of phrases that express the reality of wrongs.* Remember, silence is a phrase or multiplicity of phrases that may secretly conceal a damage, or multiple damages. The differend is an unstable state of language either covered over by silence (as when someone cannot speak, cannot find a phrase), accompanied by a feeling of pain (privation) or pleasure (when an idiom is found). At what point, one might inquire, does a damage rise to the level of being recognised as a wrong, and why should this be a concern of political philosophy in the first place?

So far, following Lyotard's sources, I have outlined the role of critical philosophy according to both the Kantian and Lyotardian descriptions: 1. the role (if not the duty) of the philosopher is to examine a given case where there is a phrase (thus, an addresser, an addressee, an object or referent), and to discriminate or make judgements by assigning phrases to their proper phrase families; and 2., where there is no precedent, invent new phrases (for example, to perform a linkage between silence, which is also a phrase, and a new phrase that includes addressor, addressee and referent). And yet, in distinction from the Kantian definition of the philosopher as judge-legislator, it would appear that Lyotard's definition of the role of the philosopher as judge would concern only those situations where the rules of precedent are completely lacking, since we recall from above that the differend appears when, even though there is a phrase (even silence is a phrase, and there are no non-phrases), there is no rule, no precedent, and thus the nature of the judgement is always 'a matter of first impression', as in common law when there exists no first phrase. This accounts for the phrase 'in this case' that constantly appears throughout concerning the finite temporality of the situation, the nature or silence of legislation and objective law on the question, and the privation or pain experienced by the plaintiff – and 'in this case' here, I am referring to the plaintiff in history as well as the contemporaneous victims in all those unknown or unheard-of cases where the legislative and executive tribunals are either silent or ambiguous concerning the existence of a differend. Accordingly, the philosopher's duty is to invent new phrases, given that 'what is at stake . . . is to bear witness to differends by finding new phrases for them', and not simply to augment for one's own benefit (scientific, economic, artistic, political, professional) the quantity of information communicable through existing phrases, but to recognise that what remains to be phrased exceeds what can presently be phrased. Although this problem of judgement is described as appearing before a particular legal tribunal, in accordance with the Kantian metaphor of the philosopher as jurist and legislator, an analogous situation of the differend can be described in aesthetic, moral and political judgement as well. This is why Lyotard questions whether the term 'faculty' can be assigned to the power of judgement, since it does not have one object, or proper phrase family, and must always resort to analogy. Therefore, concerning the exercise of judgement (which now requires the 'good linking' of heterogenous phrases), Lyotard concludes that 'a new competence (or prudence) must be found' (D: 13).

Now, granted (I admit), on first impression this seems like a very tepid definition of critical philosophy, and threatens to reduce the tribunal of critical reason to merely a 'language game' à la Wittgenstein, which is a dominant interpretation of Lyotard's own definition of the role of the philosopher. Some philosophers might immediately object – and certainly have, as Hegel did in his reading of Kant – that this is too reductive a description of the philosopher's positive discourse and role. It reduces philosophy itself to not only a quasi-juridical form of judgement, but what is worse, a judgement that is completely powerless to effectuate a rule, since it lacks, in Hegel's terminology, 'real effective negativity', what Kant would call 'executive authority', what a Marxist would call 'practical authority, and what Lyotard simply calls 'performativity'. In fact, as in the protocol of common law, the matter of first impression must await a consensual subsequent phrase, the philosopher's judgement enjoys no immediate executive or statutory authority, but awaits the consensus of another phrase that 'links to it', in which case there could be something like a first phrase, a principle, the basis for juridical law or 'right', and historically speaking, the emergence into language and sensibility the conditions of a *sensus communis*.

Nevertheless, perhaps this would be what Lyotard might call an 'ideal chaining' of phrases. In the finite situation of a differend, the philosopher judges only 'as if' judging, which either condemns the philosopher to playing a very speculative role in the name of an a priori idea of reason (as in the case of the Kantian philosopher, who, we remember, is often accused of merely being 'merely academic', like a child playing a game of draughts), or threatens the entire scene of justice becoming a farce, a Kafkaesque joke. For example, the critical tribunal could be compared to the following situation: a court hears a certain case concerning a crime of history and issues a death sentence in the name of the victims; the accused, upon hearing the sentence, is immediately let go. If this scenario could be found in Kafka, one would only need to add the following sentence: 'the condemned man, upon hearing the verdict, felt the shackles immediately drop from his body, and filled with an incredible exuberance, leapt from his box like a gymnast, and scurried out of the courtroom on all fours head over heels, in leaps and bounds, like a dog chasing a butterfly in the garden.' How would this comic presentation of the critical tribunal serve the goals of politics, much less what I have translated as the 'dignity of thinking'?

At this point, let us call before the current tribunal of political reason the differend between philosophy and the two principal adversaries that Lyotard announces as *what is at stake*: 'on its outside, the genre of economic discourse (exchange, capital); on its inside, the genre of academic discourse (mastery)' (D: xiii). Lyotard's overall argument is engaged in a struggle or battle with both these adversaries in order to save 'the honor of thinking', especially concerning the possibility of making good linkages to the problems of politics today – for example, the linking of a certain 'feeling' of a differend to the 'vigorous signs of history' that still express an enthusiasm for the idea of progress, and despite that fact that today we are often more depressed by the apparent abyss that separates our relation to this idea than enthusiastic about the prospect that we are progressing towards a better state. The problem with the external adversary of the economic genre is that 'it dismisses the occurrence, the event, the marvel, the anticipation of a community of feelings' (D: 179). This is why, as Lyotard concludes, capitalism has never constituted a universal history – in fact, it was only Marxism that provided this narrative in order to be capable of speaking about its end – but only a universal market, which it constantly defers in order to produce the gaps it needs for infinite expansion, which is substituted for any image of historical teleology (D: 179). Lyotard then criticises the first adversary under the name of liberalism by saying that it accepts the stakes of the economic genre even while priding itself on the idea of 'redistributive justice', mistaking economic exchange as the basis of the concept of political equality, and concludes that 'in principle reformism cannot make anybody happy' (referring I think to the notion of a 'happiness', individual and collective, that can only be fulfilled through a political idea of freedom).

But what about the second adversary, the one who hails from 'the inside' of philosophy itself? As an example, Lyotard speaks of 'resistance of communities bandied around their names (identities) and their narratives (cultures, information), which is counted on to stand in the way of capital's hegemony' (D: 181). 'This is a mistake,' he continues. Why a mistake? First of all, because this resistance fosters hegemony as much as it counters it (i.e., the hegemony of capitalism, or today, of 'neoliberalism'), and I do not think the continued investment in the universal narrative of Marxism has been successful in countering the economic dictatorship of human history, but has strangely consolidated its grip on the future, since it seems we cannot imagine any alternative except a post-apocalyptic future where zombies hunt down the last human beings and eat their brains. The second reason that the internal adversary is mistaken in their idea of resistance, according to Lyotard, is 'because resistance in the name of identity, culture, or community also postpones the idea of cosmopolitan history and falls back on the fear of the return of legitimation through tradition or myth (fascism, racism, etc.)' (D: 181).

What Lyotard identifies as a common trait in both adversaries is the suspension of a cosmopolitan idea of human history as a final end (the idea of 'progress' or continual improvement of practical political reason), which is indefinitely deferred by the external adversary of economic thinking, and presumptuously postponed (or suspended) by the internal adversary in order to defend against the return of archaic and religious sources of authority such as sovereignty or ethnocentric community. In either case, there is always the temptation for the critical tribunal of political reason to simply accept the current state of affairs in place of a final end of political reason and become a real politico-juridical tribunal that has the performative powers to effectuate the reality of its own legitimation protocols (i.e., in many ways, to function exactly like the historical-political tribunal that appears in the farce by Zinoviev). For example, this would be the form of the legitimation protocol that governs the reality of judgement in the so-called 'post-truth' regime.

Towards a New Philosophical *Bildungsroman*

Concluding my brief reflections on the archipelago of political reason today, I would remind you once again that the cause of the 'differend' is a feeling (of pain or privation), 'in this case', the privation felt by the imagination first for the idea of progress towards a better state of political reason, leading to either capitulation or to the pathological feeling of disillusionment (or, again, worse, to a spirit of revenge against 'Time and its It Was', to quote Nietzsche). Concerning the idea of the end of human history, Lyotard concludes the 1981 lecture on the Kantian Critique of History by invoking the Kantian definition of 'culture' as the aptitude to 'propose for oneself the ends in general' (E: 67). This aptitude, capacity or simply 'power' is not aesthetic in a narrow understanding (the cultivation of a formal sensibility or taste in the realm of art in analogy with the laws of nature), nor the ethical-moral *sensus communis* (the agreement of individual will and law, or the principles virtue with the ethical sensibility), but also refers also to a 'political culture' whose final end is universal cosmopolitanism. Thus, the concept of culture must include a 'trace of freedom in reality', which serves to 'edify' and to cultivate the individual and the collective will, that is, the trace of a supersensible idea that cannot be found in nature, which is the idea of a perfectibility of taste, knowledge, judgement and virtue. In Kant's late writings, especially the 'Conjectures on the Beginning of Human History', as Lyotard observes, the 'manner' in which the trace of this idea is expressed is the *Bildungsroman*, in the critical sense of the 'cultivation of the will' and the 'disciplining of desire' in all the above senses – aesthetic, ethico-moral, and practical or political (and perhaps even sexual?).

In response, I will note that it seems odd for the 'postmodern theorist who declared the end of all master narratives' to introduce again, it seems, at the end of history, the usefulness of a certain *novel* that will either serve to edify or to destroy the trace of the idea of progress toward of a universal destination of politics. Of course, the 'object' of the universal community of reasonable beings. (**Note:** *I do not employ the*

Kantian concept of humanity for this 'object', or rather 'subject', since the definition of 'who qualifies as a reasonable being?' is a historico-political idea, just like whether Ibanskian is a communist – and cannot belong to the historical-political reality of one culture alone, or perhaps even one species being!) To illustrate this according to the fable of providence that Kant employs, nature would not be predisposed to locate the idea of the final end in the historical-political reality in only one portion of humankind, and then to destine the cultivation of the idea to the rest of the world through a colonisation of all culture. Of course, I realise that this is how the Kantian idea of culture and reason has often been read by the antagonists of the idea of providence, which is often accused of secretly harbouring a Eurocentric and Christian historical-political *Bildungsroman*.

Nevertheless, as 'is the case' with any work of fiction, a particular *Bildungsroman* can either be edifying and practically useful or not, in which case it can easily be dismissed out of hand as 'mere fiction', 'a sweet dream' (as in the case of the idea of perpetual peace), or worse, can be utilised in calculative reasoning as propagandistic ideology. In 'The End of All Things' (1784) from which Lyotard derives his reading of two novels of culture that recount both the beginning and the end of all things, thus combining the omens from the youngest of days (*jüngster Tag*) with the signs of revelation of the end of days, he does find one novel more useful (favourable), and the other novel perverse to an extreme degree (damning). Ultimately, the problem of the *Bildungsroman* of Christian Europe, according to Kant, is that

> in the natural progress of the human race, talents, skills, tastes (along with its result, voluptuousness [the feeling of satisfaction that accompanies the achievement of a desired end in all the above activities]) become cultivated before morality develops, and this state is the most burdensome and dangerous one possible for morality, as well as for physical well-being, for needs grow much more vigorously than do the means to satisfy them. (PP: 96)

As Kant says in *The Principles of Politics*, however, it is because human nature is made up of such bent material, it is first in the realm of culture that certain final ends are attained, even while moral culture always lags miserably behind. What can be made straight in the area of culture can only provide 'tools' for disciplining the moral and practical will, twisted by self-interest, power and oppression, pain and sadness, and so on. At the same time, as in the case of the beautiful, culture can only offer us a 'consolation', and thus the importance of the experience of the sublime is that it can either directly *invigorate* the moral and political will (even at the price of the pain inflicted on the imagination and the understanding) or, as a modification of the subjective disposition of self-affection, can also threaten the faculties with the worse pain and a complete loss of vitality. This is precisely the source of Lyotard's use of the terms 'weariness' (*lassitude*) and even 'the miserable exhaustion' (*relâchement*) to define the predominant 'feeling' of the academic discourse of postmodern theory in his day, that is, the internal adversary of philosophising. I would say that this 'feeling' has only grown more dominant of late and may even be called pathological, that is, as a permanent modification of the subject of philosophy itself, which may be nearly close to extinction.

In the *Conjectures*, Kant explicitly warned against the dangers of this 'feeling' – we could say, a historical feeling of a differend – that is common among reflective and sensitive people, especially philosophers of his day. He writes: 'The reflective person feels a grief that the unreflective do not know, a grief that can well lead to moral ruin: this is the discontentedness with the providence that governs the entire course of the world; and he feels it when he thinks about the evil that so greatly oppresses the human race, leaving it without (apparent) hope for something better' (PP: 57). If there is no remedy in culture, this will lead to a subjective status that Kant will call 'perverse', providing as examples the insane asylum and a certain gnostic creation fable from Zoroastrianism concerning the fall of Adam and Eve from paradise; or, in fact, their expulsion to Earth which is described by the angel as 'a latrine for the whole universe' (PP: 97). For example, Kant writes, in imagining the end of all things, that:

> some only see signs of increasing injustice, oppression of the poor by wanton revelry of the rich, and the universal loss of honesty and faith, or in bloody wars in which the entire Earth is enflamed, and so on; in other words people see signs in a moral collapse and in the rapid rise of all vices, along with their accompanying evils, of the sort that they fancy previous times they have never seen [here, I think, Kant is referring to the creation of utopian novels of human history that narrate the fall as the state of current things, if not their eternity]. Still others see signs in unaccustomed changes in unaccustomed natural changes, in earthquakes, in storms, in floods, or in comets and atmospheric signs [e.g., the same signs we are reading today in the contemporary novel of the Anthropocene].

What is remarkable about both the above observations that Kant is making concerning his own philosophical culture – perhaps he was reading pessimistic Rousseau following the Lisbon earthquake? – is that we are still reading the same novels or *Bildungsromane*, or at least some version thereof concerning the same signs of history (for example, the novels of Agamben, or the pulp fiction of Žižek regarding the 'End of All Things'). If the novel is the form that is peculiar to human cultures so to impose a sensuous structure on these very conditions to organise or structure our experience of the a priori conditions of space and time, then our capacity or incapacity to imagine a better state of things is dependent on this primitive technological tool first employed by religions, later by philosophy (beginning with Hegel), and today by the *Bildungsroman* that has over the last century or so has gone by the name of 'critical theory'. Therefore, as Lyotard argues, not only do we need to develop a 'a new competence (or prudence)' in order to bear witness to the differend, but we also need an entirely new *Bildungsroman* as well. The philosophy of *The Differend* remains only an initial sketch or a map that looks like it has been drawn by a child – we must imagine each numbered article has a different colour, and the whole book would resemble those round globes in elementary school with brightly coloured territories. With regard to the 'mood' (*Stimmung*) that predominates in Lyotard's late political writings, it is certainly not hopeful, but rather a feeling of 'vigorous melancholy'. It is for this reason that in the closing of *The Differend* (which simply lapses into silence, rather than actually concludes), Lyotard asks: 'Would a vigorously melancholic humanity be sufficient thereby to supply the proof that "it is progressing toward the better"?' (D: 179).

The question that should concern us is the following: what is the mood that is proper or 'fitting' for philosophy today: the calculated optimism of Kant (which has often been accused of being too Christian), or the vigorous melancholy of Lyotard (which has been called too pagan or stoic)? In some ways this is a ridiculous question; one cannot choose one's own particular mood, and certainly not one's existential mood, which belongs to 'no one and everyone' (recalling the subtitle of Nietzsche's *Thus Spoke Zarathustra*). No one can possess a feeling that belongs only to themselves, since it must be possible for everyone to feel the same thing – at least, *en potentia* – which is why the particular feeling that belongs to a differend is at the same time the condition of its communicability, even *sensus communis*. This feeling is evident in Lyotard's conclusion to *The Differend* concerning the postmodern philosophy of his time:

'PHILOSOPHY IS DEAD!

'THE TIME HAS COME TO PHILOSOPHISE!' (D: 181)

Of course, sometimes the feeling of exhaustion is mistaken for manic exuberance, which makes perfect sense from a psychological point of view; it is from the deepest depression that either one turns to the promise of the end of all things (e.g., 'the Anthropocene', species extinction, ecological holocaust, the end of capitalism, etc., etc.), or what amounts to the same feeling from a manic disposition, desperately craving for the new *this*, the new *that*, or the post-*this*, the post *that* (e.g., new materialism, posthumanism, or 'the post-critical', etc., etc.). Returning to Lyotard's original description, the second clause was translated as a ';period of slackening', but the French term *relâchement* can perhaps be better rendered by 'relaxation', or 'decontraction', both of which bear an essentially Bergsonian image of duration as the most expanded or decontracted duration of the past. As Gilles Deleuze summarised this extremely important ontological proposition by Bergson:

> While the past co-exists with its own present, and while it coexists with itself on various levels of contraction, we must recognize that the present itself is only the most contracted level of the past . . . just as indeterminate matter (i.e. extension, space) is the most relaxed (*detendu*) degree of the present). (D: 74)

It is this continuous duration between memory, as the most contracted state of the past (i.e., recollection of the present), and matter, as the most decontracted state of the present (i.e., extension), which explains the feeling that 'we' can coexist in the same present in analogy to the manner in which we can co-inhabit a common space, even though this feeling is itself a purely subjective illusion. This is why, in my previous writings on contemporary philosophy, I refer to what Bergson identifies as 'a reflective faculty' underlying the multiple and divergent points of view that determine the present through the recollection and anticipation of the past, thus producing a vital image of duration in both its phases of contraction and expansion or decontraction.[1] According to the same Bergsonian analogy, we might grasp the composition of particular traits in a number of 'new thises' and 'post-thats' that belong to the duration of contemporary philosophy. Nevertheless, underlying this series one can easily detect a dominant affective mood, which Lyotard earlier diagnosed as 'weariness' (*lassitude*), as if the present we are co-inhabiting is already growing old, and even despite the frenetic number of new analytical positions and contrary to the recent claims that we have leaped beyond our past and exist now in a period marked by the exuberance and anticipation (e.g., 'These are exciting times in our field . . .', 'There has never been a better time to be young', etc.).

Perhaps the above sentiment only expresses 'my feeling', my differend, even though, according to the same argument, it cannot be my feeling alone. (Remember, even silence expresses a differend, or should I say, every silence bears a differend whose open universe awaits what Lyotard calls '*le "bon" enchaînement*' [D: xiv].) Moreover, according to my calendar, the present we are currently inhabiting belongs to the same continuous duration of the 'post-critical' that emerged at the end of the 1970s, a present that has lasted almost forty years! (As an aside, this is exactly the same amount of time that the Israelites wandered through the desert after the incident at Mount Horeb.) And I wonder if we are even now seeing the end or edge of our own desert? Of course, I remain sceptical, but to rephrase this according to what I have called 'the return address', the contemporary programme of the 'post-critical [aka 'post-Kantian] philosophy' is a return statement that is now over forty years running, and rather than announcing its end, the function of the dominant return statements in contemporary philosophy today can actually be measured in terms of their success in 'saving more time' (*gagner le temps*).

Still, there is something new! As Lyotard also observed in the context of the emergence of 'our present', what is new is the use of time itself that reigns today in every public space – including, I do not need to add, the space of contemporary philosophy and/or theory. For example, some thought that the philosophies of the new digital media would naturally be able to resist this market logic, but, ironically, have only turned out to be its major innovators, even though its most prolific pioneers have not benefited professionally. Of course, this is not their fault, and there has been a strange schism between academic publishing and the disciplinary regime of philosophy in the academy during the same period. (In so-called 'public space', including academic publishing, it is the finality of the economic genre that determines the value of every new statement.) On the other hand, if an author attempts to write a book of philosophy that announces its intention up front is not to fashion a new statement – thus it will serve absolutely no use for the reader in 'saving more time' – does this afford a minimal space for critical reflection on our 'our own time'? *Perhaps only time will tell.* In the meantime, instead of seeking a point of conviction or certainty, I choose to follow Lyotard into the present, that is, *to remain 'rigorously melancholy'.* In my view, we have not yet learned to become melancholy enough! Here, I might also recall Kant's famous mantra *Sapere aude!* which can be variously translated 'Have courage!' or 'Dare to know!' And I say this especially to the aforementioned 'young': don't be fooled by all the new slogans in contemporary philosophy, or, in other words, 'Dare to be critical!' Therefore, in concluding my own private reflections on our contemporary *Bildungsroman*, I will simply defer to a conceptual persona who appears in the last pages of *The Differend*, but who seems to express a new feeling of courage, or 'critical attitude', which is described in the following statement: 'he only knows that this ignorance [concerning what counts for useful knowledge today] is the ultimate resistance of the event [of thinking] that can be opposed to any accountable [*comptable*] use of time' (D: 15).

Note

1. See Lambert, *Return Statements.*

Part II:
On the Pedagogy of Concepts

4. 'Another Person' (*Autrui*)

In the history of philosophy, concepts are only created as a function of problems that are adequately expressed and the corresponding concepts can be either well-made or horribly botched. Consequently, all concepts are connected to problems without which they would have no meaning and which can themselves only be isolated or understood as their solution emerges. In order to discern the difference between a well-made or badly botched concept requires what Deleuze calls 'a pedagogy of the concept', which is a reflective discipline that must be added artificially to the history of philosophy. As Deleuze explains, 'philosophers introduce new concepts, they explain them, but they don't tell us, not completely anyway, the problems to which the concepts are a response' (N: 136).

In taking up the concept of 'another person' (*autrui*), we are presented with a problem concerning the plurality of subjects, their relationship, and their reciprocal presentations. The problem is determining under what specific conditions the concept of the subject comes first, if not absolutely, but in relation to another subject. That is to say, is the concept of another person necessarily always second in relation to a subject or a self? If so, it is to the extent that its concept is that or another – a subject that presents itself as an object – which is special in relation to the self: they are two components. However, if the other person is identified with a special object, it is now only the other subject as it appears to me; and if we identify it with another subject, it is me who is the other person as I appear to that subject. Of course, everything changes if we think that we discover another problem, which is the special nature of another person when he or she appears to me as a special object in the perceptual field of the subject, or likewise, when I appear as another person from the perspective of another subject. From this we must conclude that the other person requires an a priori concept from which the special object, the other subject and the self must all derive, not the other way around. The order has changed, as has the nature of the concepts and the problems to which they are supposed to resolve. Whether or not another person can be qualified as an a priori concept, or a category, is the problem I will address below through the conceptual solutions offered by Deleuze and Sartre. Although it might appear odd, upon first glance, to propose the question of 'the other person' in the form of 'What is . . .?' (*ti esti*), this is because the entity in question is not subjectively determined, but rather is the concept of a transcendental impersonal field that exists prior to a subject ('the self') or a special object ('the other'). In perhaps the most remarkable pages towards the end of *Difference and Repetition*, in the conclusion of the chapter on 'The Asymmetrical Synthesis of the Sensible', Deleuze identifies another person as the presence of an a priori structure that testifies to the existence of a 'center of envelopment' that belong to psychic systems. 'These centers are clearly constituted neither by the I nor by the Self, but by a completely different structure belonging to the I–Self system' (DR: 260). What Deleuze at this point calls a 'structure', and designates with the term 'autrui', refers only to the self for the other I and the other I for the self. Therefore, as Deleuze argues, when the 'other' is understood to be secondary to the self or the subject ('reduced to the status of an object from the pole it assumes the status of a subject', that is, to a 'disqualified subject', or a 'special object'), its real function has been misunderstood by the history of the concept – including the philosophy of Sartre, who as Deleuze argues elsewhere, was the first to recognise this structure in the pages of the *Transcendence of the Ego*, but then in *Being and Nothingness* reduces it to represent an aspect of the gaze.

But what happens when, following Deleuze, we recognise the structure of another person only by its purely formal character (qua 'Other'), that is to say by its expressive value: as the expression of the other I for the self and, at the same time, of the self for the other I? In other words, as a centre of envelopment that is imbricated with in two psychic systems? The other is no one really. No subject can occupy the other, but only as the other I for the self. The structure actually testifies to the reversibility of psychic systems, as well as the possibility of their *resonance*, *imbrication*, *explication* and *envelopment*. As Deleuze writes, 'the Other thus functions as a center of enwinding, envelopment or implication' (DR: 261). Moreover, if the Other functions as a centre of envelopment that already belongs to the I–Self system, then the I and the self are only the functions of explication or development and correspond to the values of individuation of psychic systems. Furthermore, the 'I' and the 'self' are not themselves centres of individuation within the two psychic systems, but rather functions of extensive development of what is implicated in each system. The Other is the envelopment of individuation as an expressive value, while the I and the self are the development of individuation as extensive values, and 'they always tend to develop and explicate the world expressed by others'. All this goes to say that Deleuze reverses the direction of priority: the Other is the expression of the possible world, and there is no possible world without the expression of the Other, the subject and the self being only developments of relations that were already implicated in the possibility of an a priori and impersonal structure.

In order to grasp the Other in its a priori nature, Deleuze immediately insists that this can only be accomplished in special conditions of experience, however artificial, and only when the expressed has no existence apart from what expresses it. In order to illustrate this special condition, Deleuze resorts to a specific scene that I will return to again several times: a terrified face, which expresses a terrifying world, but in a state of envelopment. For example, upon glimpsing the face, the subject could turn around, but this possibility is first given from the position of the other person, since the face bears no resemblance to the cause of the terror that is revealed. Yet, the fact that it now exists as a possible world for the subject (a world of fear) is already owed to the reversibility of the Other as structure. Even if the source of the terror is not physical, but psychical, as in the statement 'I'm afraid', this becomes the point of explication and language (i.e., expression).

Let us now turn to the opening of *What is Philosophy?* where the concept returns again and, at this point, is offered as the first example or illustration of what is called a concept in philosophy, since the history of this concept is exemplary of the problem solving character to which the creation of concepts belongs. Once again, here we encounter the same problem: 'Is another person necessarily second in relation to the self? Under what specific conditions do we often begin with the concept of a subject or a self from which the other person is derived as a secondary self or as the form of the subject?' What is the problem to which these questions respond? In fact, at this point, Deleuze states the problem quite explicitly: 'we are dealing with the problem concerning the plurality of subjects, their relationship, and the reciprocal presentation' (WP:

16). Therefore, everything changes if we begin with the other person first, which requires an a priori concept from which the special object, the other subject and the self all derive. And yet, we should note that *autrui* is not described as a structure this time, but remains the name of a centre of envelopment, which envelopes the special object, the other subject and the self as its necessary components. 'In this sense, it is a concept with three inseparable components: possible world, existing face, and real language or speech' (WP: 17). In other words, the change in order now corresponds to a new problem: not the I as subject, which is reduced purely to a 'linguistic index' (a Piercean sign), but the Other as a centre of envelopment.

At this point, a new problem suddenly appears, which is the presupposition of the a priori character that is now ascribed to the concept of *autrui* as such? This presupposes that an a priori concept of the Other exists, and presuming that no such concept yet exists, given how the problems and terms were previously ordered where the concept of the subject always comes or is posited first, then a new concept must now be invented or created in order to express this character. Here, I would argue, we might also detect a little humour in Deleuze's use of the concept of the *autrui* as the first example of what is called s concept in philosophy. Why? Because we have just established that the concept does not yet exist, or still needs to be created or invented to resolve the problem of the a priori nature of others (even before this becomes a problem of amphibology). However, what the concept does illustrate is the manner in which philosophy solves problems by means of inventing new concepts, or by fixing earlier ones that were poorly made. In this case, the solution is quite simple: reverse the order of placing the other person first, that is, before the I and the self, and everything is suddenly reoriented. In fact, it's a brilliant move, as an analytic philosopher might exclaim. Even more importantly, as Deleuze now argues, 'the creation of the concept of the Other person with these components will now entail the creation of a new concept of perceptual space' (WP: 19). How so?

Before answering this question, first we must ask what it means when a philosopher says that he can create or invent an a priori concept as one manner of resolving a problem of philosophy, in this case, specifically the problem of the plurality of subjects, their relationships and their reciprocal presentation? By what kind of right can a philosopher make this claim, given that we might suppose that a priori concepts already exist, and the philosopher's role is relegated to discovering them like buried treasure. What is an a priori concept? Simply put, an a priori concept is a species of concepts that a philosopher can lay claim to 'by a kind of right', as Deleuze and Guattari will also say in the conclusion concerning the competition between philosophy and its modern rivals. As Deleuze himself argues elsewhere, the notion of right cannot be founded on anything other than itself; there is a concept of right, to be sure, as well as a philosophy of right, but the actual claim to right leads to an infinite regression: the subject of right must already have the right to claim it in principle, and often this takes the form of innateness. Freedom, for example, is an innate right of the subject who claims it, who performs this right to have rights qua being a subject of rights. Moreover, innateness refers to an essence, a substantial or inclusive predicate of the subject of right. Therefore, the right to the concept – and particularly, I will argue, certain a priori concepts – is a claim that belongs essentially (or innately) to philosophical statements. In other words, if we cannot think of philosophy, in both its modern and ancient sense, in its Greek and German and even French traditions, without a priori concepts, it is because of this unique property of the philosophical enunciation that the philosopher can lay claim to them; especially, given also the fact that certain concepts are a priori concepts cannot be proven from experience, or after experience, which is why they must either be deduced or invented to solve a particular problem. As Deleuze will say, even empiricism had to invent new concepts in order to propose the priority of perception over the innateness of ideas.

There is always a slippage in Deleuze's account between an idea and a concept, but this is owed to the treatment of these terms in the history of philosophy, which has two principal sources: the Platonic theory of recollection concerning innate ideas, and the Kantian deduction of pure concepts of reason concerning a priori synthetic concepts, which are the necessary conditions of all possible experience. Throughout Deleuze's account of the other person as the condition of a possible world, it is clear he is not referring to an idea that exists innately in our experience of other people, in which case the plurality of our relations to others would occur as the abstraction of a predicate that already belongs to the other person, as a genus, or to a class of others in general. However, the a priori nature of the concept cannot be thought through the identity of a predicate as in the example 'all men are mortal', and so the class of judgement is synthetic in which the connection is thought without identity – in this case, between the 'I', another subject, and a special object.

If we recall the Kantian exposition of the specific nature of a priori concepts from the *Critique of Pure Reason*, there we immediately find the claim that any knowledge of a priori concepts must be combined with 'spontaneity', since both identity and universality are judgements that are combined with spontaneity and it is by their means alone that an object is conferred with an objective reality. Therefore, spontaneity is the common trait of three syntheses: the synthesis of apprehension in intuition, the synthesis of reproduction in imagination, and the synthesis of recognition in the concept. However, it is only in the instance of the third synthesis of spontaneity with receptivity that the specific objective reality of a concept is made possible, because without either the spontaneous receptivity of intuition or recognition concepts could not appear as such. To paraphrase Kant, it is only after we have 'produced' this third synthesis that we can say *there is an object* = *x*. This, in turn, leads Kant to posit the idea of a transcendental apprehension, which is the ground of all concepts, but especially of objectivity as such as also the condition of the possibility of any object whatsoever (i.e., *object* = *x*). Thus, the possibility of objectivity in general is conditioned by the possible apprehension of an object, the conditioned and the condition are given a symmetrical formulation, and the apprehension of the object is conditioned by the production of the third synthesis: there is no knowledge of the object that does not arrive by concepts, and concepts are necessary and serve as the universal rule for the appearance of objects in general (*object* = *x*). Nevertheless, we must acknowledge that even in Kant the existence of this object must be deduced before it can be experienced, and has the same character of a problem that is resolved by the invention of an a priori concept in order to solve the problem of identity between the object of intuition, imagination and understanding arrived at through concepts, in the manner of giving each of these syntheses a common sense, an original sociability, or accord among the faculties. I have highlighted this moment in Kant's deduction simply to call attention to this problem solving aspect we also observed when Deleuze must deduce the existence of an a priori concept of the other person in the same manner, and by means of a spontaneous and transcendental apprehension.

Once again let us recall also that the chapter in which the a priori concept of the other person first appears in Deleuze's philosophy is titled 'the asymmetrical synthesis of the sensible', in which we might conclude the addition of a fourth synthesis added to the Kantian architectonic plan. In the discussion of this fourth synthesis, at the end of which the a priori concept of the other person is claimed to be both necessary and universal, as the condition of the plurality of subjects and their reciprocal presentations, the event of a spontaneous apprehension is highlighted as well in the sudden appearance of a face, and some words, which confer objective reality to the possible world. In this case, the relation between apprehension and spontaneity is said to be asymmetrical, rather than symmetrical in the sense of centred by the same object or the same I. It is this asymmetrical character that seems to appear in the judgement that the other person is not identical with another subject, nor with the special object. As Deleuze writes, 'even while he refuses a logical extension to space and time, Kant's mistake is to maintain a geometrical extension for it, . . . an *external relation* with extensity as a whole of form of extensive magnitude' (DR: 231). It is here that Deleuze identifies the 'paradox of symmetrical objects' (i.e., right and left, high and low, figure and ground) which is given an intensive source and a transcendental principle that is not merely an anticipation of perception (according to a temporal synthesis) but rather a fourfold genesis of extension in the form of schema: *extensity* in the form of extensive magnitude, *qualitas* in the form of matter occupying extensity, and, lastly, the *quale* in the form of designation of an object (i.e., *object* = *x*). But what does this have to do with the concept of the other person (*autrui*)? Very early on Deleuze highlights the fact that this 'paradox of symmetrical objects' is in fact introduced by another subject in the perceptual field (for whom my right side corresponds to his or her left); or, more accurately, the other subject comes to occupy a position in the perceptual field of the I that is already structured by a differential relation, such that it makes possible (and conditions) the empirical experience of dissymmetry between the I and the Other, but which, in turn, becomes a strange form of symmetry. The problem introduces what Deleuze constantly highlights is the 'strange oscillation' that often occurs around the position of the other person when the subject is posited first: the Other oscillates between the pole of another subject and a special object; however, this oscillation itself must occur already to the intensive coordination of a *spatium* that exists prior, making possible the extensive difference between left and right, front and behind, inside and outside, and so on.

At this point, I will now turn to the passage where Deleuze states this problem (or this misunderstanding) explicitly:

> Theories tend to oscillate mistakenly and ceaselessly from a pole at which the other is reduced to the status of object at a pole at which it assumes the status of a subject. Even Sartre was content to inscribe this oscillation in the other as such, in showing that the other became other when I became subject, and did not become subject unless I in turn became object. As a result, the structure of the other, as well as its role in psychic systems, remained misunderstood. (DR: 260)

In the case of these theories in which the Other oscillates between these two poles, the problem is that this already presupposes the forms of the object and subject are given prior to the appearance of the other person. The form of the subject already encloses or totalises the perceptual field in which others appear. The mistake in this formulation is the positing of a simultaneity of object and subject in the supposed same perceptual field; for example, from what perspective could the other person appear as the same time, from one perspective, an object in my perceptual field, and from another simultaneously, as another subject gazing at me? In real experience, there is no such perspective belonging to the perceptual field itself and the fundamental mistake is to posit this oscillation in the form of simultaneity. I cannot occupy at the same time – that is to say, simultaneously – the position both of the object and a subject. 'The mistake of theories of knowledge is that they postulate the contemporaneity of subject and object, whereas one is constituted only through the annihilation of the other' (LS: 310). In traditional theories of the subject, this mistaken contemporaneity of subject and object appears in the form of dualism, as the above-mentioned oscillation between object and another subject, distorting the reality of how things actually appear in perception, when in fact it should be expressed as a temporal distinction between consciousness and its object. 'The Other thus assures the distinction of consciousness and its object as a temporal distinction', thus creating the conditions (as Deleuze says 'the bridge') for one perceptual field to pass into another, to become, to enter a becoming through the redistribution of its elements, including the self, the object and the other subject (LS: 311).

What is the source of this strange oscillation itself that reduces others sometimes to objects or to other subjects. According to traditional theories, it is the form of the I that becomes identified with the source of this oscillation; it is from the position of the I that others are reduced to the status of objects or recognised as other subjects belonging to the same perceptual field. But what if, in fact, it were the other way around and it was from the position of the other person that this oscillation ensues, but not only between objective and subjective poles, but in entirely different dimensions that involve points of envelopment and differential relations of extensive magnitude.

> No longer subject of the field or object in the field, the other person will become the condition under which not only subject and object are redistributed but also figure and ground, margin and center, moving object and reference point, transitive and substantial, length and depth, etc. . . . For example, the Other person is enough to make any length a possible depth in space, and *vice versa*, so that if this concept did not function in the perceptual field, transitions and inversions would become incomprehensible, and we would always run up against things . . . (WP: 18–19)

To employ a simple illustration, in passing through a room I walk by certain pieces of furniture, which I avoid by walking around them, as well as corners and obstructions, immovable objects; suddenly, in the next moment, I turn around and head for the door I entered, remembering the furniture I just walked around. Without the categorical function of the other person, I would have no memory and trip over the coffee table. Thus, this expresses the temporal function of the structure; the other person causes time to undergo a redistribution of its dimensions between what comes before and what comes after the present 'Now'. In the absence of the other person, Deleuze writes, there is no longer a distinction between consciousness and its object, which are now one. The room I just walked into is frozen eternally in time; moreover, the consciousness merges with the room and settles on the furniture like dust. There is no past I with regard to the present moment of consciousness, no possible transition into another I since the category of the other person is missing or absent. It is only in this moment that 'I = I', as Sartre also argued, but this I would be empty and abstract, or purely formal and transcendental. It is, in fact, the possibility that language affords which there is no temporal distinction between the I and the object, but rather consciousness clings to the object like a phosphorescent covering; the object is illuminated by consciousness, in a language which appears almost to speak itself: a language of pure impersonal being or consciousness of the I.

In this regard, as Deleuze says, it is perhaps Sartre who went furthest in discovering the structure of the Other as a condition of real experience, and not only possible or formal experience that determines our knowledge of objects. This becomes not only his critique of the formal character of transcendental subject in Kant and Husserl, but also of Hegel and Heidegger (even though he will argue that it is Hegel, not Heidegger, who offers us some progress after Husserl). Deleuze pays homage to Sartre's concept of the other person from the chapter of *Being and Nothingness*, 'The Existence of Others', even though he will say that Sartre also the concept in the final analysis of the gaze that reintroduces this strange oscillation between the other as object in the perceptual field, or subject of the perceptual field. Because I think this is a crucial point, I will spend some time with Sartre's description before turning to Deleuze's response. First of all, as we recall, philosophy always proceeds by means of concepts in a problem-solving manner; the problem that Sartre is constantly evoking and attempting to resolve is solipsism. Consequently, in order to resolve this problem, an adequate concept of the Other's existence is required, which would not be purely formal or reduce the Other to the condition of an object of knowledge. This is because the subject's relation to others does not, first of all, concern the relation of knowledge, even though it is the basis for the subject's relation of knowledge of the world populated by objects and by other subjects. For Sartre, the Other introduces a distinction between consciousness and its object, but one that cannot be represented by our knowledge of objects.

In perhaps the most dense and beautiful section of his meditation on the existence of others, Sartre thus recounts the history of the concept in order to surpass it and to avoid the dangerous reef of solipsism. The problem of solipsism, the apparent negation of others as necessary to my experience, the ability of the self to become 'for itself', to an extreme degree that occasions a withdrawal from the world constituted by others and the possibility of maliciousness and evil – can only exist in a world that is already conditioned by the presence of others. As Levinas will also argue, and also in response to the concept of the Other in Sartre, the subject cannot give to itself its own nothingness; the very negativity that defines solipsism, solitude and withdrawal into the ego is given first of all made possible by the existence of others. It is only in relation to all the others that I am alone, singular and unique; that I have these possibilities as my freedom and my flight. To annihilate the Other is, therefore, to negate the very possibility that 'I am I'. Perhaps a stronger way of putting this is that the subject does not constitute out of its own nothingness, or from its own alienation (*ekstasis*), the possibility of others – that is to say, the subject cannot find in its own existence an a priori structure of experience that is valid for itself as well as for others.

This critique that we can find in both the philosophies of Sartre and Levinas is directed against Heidegger's concept of *Dasein*'s transcendence as 'being towards death', which Sartre accuses as being a form of 'bad faith', and Levinas says is 'guilty' of eliding the priority of the Other's existence. According to Sartre, there is a 'devious reasoning' at work in Heidegger's concept of *ekstasis*, which he sometimes takes as being 'outside of self toward self' and sometimes as being 'outside of self in others', though in a manner that the first sense slides into the second and becomes the only authentic form of *ekstasis*, whereas Sartre finds these two forms of alienation strictly incompatible (i.e., asymmetrical), and it is around this point that we also find the essence of Levinas's critique that the subject cannot 'give to itself' the ecstatic moment of being outside oneself in others. As Sartre concludes,

> Heidegger's attempt to bring human reality out of its solitude raises those same difficulties which idealism generally encounters when it tries to establish the existence of concrete beings which are similar to us and which as such escape our experience, which even as they are being constituted do not arise from our a priori. (BN: 336)

Therefore, after rejecting Heidegger's concept of ecstatic temporality of *Dasein* as a being emerging out of its own solitude as *Dasein*, he concludes with a fundamental insight: 'Human-reality [*Dasein*] remains alone because the Other's existence has the nature of a contingent and irreducible fact. We encounter the Other; we do not constitute him' (BN: 336).

But what does it mean when Sartre discovers, on the basis of his rejection of Heidegger's concept of *Dasein*, that the Other is both contingent and yet necessary, even though the form of necessity here is not ontological, which is to say that it does not belong to those conditions of the possibility of experience in the same manner as objects? Here, Sartre is denying to the Other the status of a category; thus, the Other is a 'contingent necessity, the same kind of factual necessity that is imposed upon the cogito' (BN: 337). The Other has the same character of 'contingent facticity' that is present in the apodictic existence of the cogito itself, as a form of indubitability that is always open to the possibility of doubt, which opens the cogito to unending reflection of its own substance in thought, in the same sense that the Other's 'irreducible facticity' is contingent, meaning that its existence is always open to the possibility of absence or negation. 'If the Other's existence is not a vain conjecture, a pure fiction, it is because there is a sort of cogito concerning it' (BN: 338). As in the case of Hegel, we are thrown back onto the cogito itself as an irreducible limit to our access to the Other in his subjectivity. 'In a word my only point of departure is the interiority of the cogito' (BN: 329) and even if the interiority of the Other we posit another cogito, then this interiority will be in its facticity another interiority that is outside my own, just as I am outside the interiority constituted by the other person who is thus determined as another subject like me. There is no way to prove this, no manner of establishing the coincidence of the Other's interiority as being identical with my own, no manner of establishing with certainty of knowledge that at the deepest point of these two interiorities: I is I, or I = I. In a word, again, they remain irreducibly asymmetrical and 'between the Other-as-object and Me-as-subject there is no common measure, no more than between self-consciousness and consciousness of the Other' (BN: 328).

It now appears that we have reached an impasse once again, or what Sartre refers to as an 'ontological divide', and I have continuously remarked as an asymmetrical moment in the analytic of self and the other. And yet, there is a solution to this impasse that is already established by Descartes himself, and returns again in Hegel by default: since the cogito is our only point of departure, I must 'go through' the cogito as the only means of 'establishing the ground of that factual necessity of the Other's existence, but not by revealing to me an a priori structure that would point to an equally a priori Other', as Descartes did in the Fifth Meditation by positing God as the condition of closure and of a common sense of consciousness. Therefore, instead of establishing between subject and the Other a transcendental form of symmetry that apprehends me and the other at the same time, Sartre upholds a relation that can only appear asymmetrical in that the concrete existence of the Other expresses as a condition of its For-Itself the revelation of my own concrete and contingent existence, which has the character of facticity and immanence. 'Thus, we must ask the For-Itself to deliver to us the For-Others; we must ask absolute immanence to throw us into absolute transcendence' (BN:

338). Perhaps this final statement, which represents Sartre's solution of the impasse presented by the no exit of the cogito, we might indeed expect that Deleuze would part company, since one does not manage to pass though absolute immanence only to arrive (back) at absolute transcendence. Or perhaps we must hear this sentence in the form of a prayer: 'Oh Lord, we ask the For-Itself to deliver us from the For-Others! We ask pure immanence to throw us into absolute transcendence!' Here, with this statement which appears immediately before a break in Sartre's long meditation on the history of the concept of the Other – a history in which Hegel comes after Husserl and Heidegger, by the way! – and then the introduction of a new series of concepts around the structure of the 'look' (the gaze), we might suspect there is a sudden speculative leap that cuts the Gordian knot that Sartre has just spent the previous twenty pages tying so tightly, that is to say, the knot that he already determined as the 'ontological divide' between my consciousness and the consciousness of the Other. In fact, we would not be wrong in our suspicion and immediately find a leap in the extension of the cogito to the apodicticity of the Other's existence as a fact. In other words, Sartre simply extends the form of the cogito to the expression of the problem of the Other in order to establish as the ground of both the cogito and the Other a contingent and yet irreducible facticity. The facticity of the cogito is expressed in the statement 'I am', a statement that immediately expresses the fact of existence. Likewise, the facticity of the Other is expressed in the statement 'there is', or 'there are others', a statement that immediately (or spontaneously) expresses the existence of the Other who is also the fact of my existence for the Other. 'The Cartesian cogito makes an affirmation of the absolute truth of a fact – that of my existence. In the same way that the cogito, a little expanded as we are using it here, reveals to us as a fact the existence of the Other and my existence for the Other' (BN: 376). On both occasions, 'it is true that my being-for-others and my consciousness of being has the character of an absolute event'. But again, it is not as an event that takes place once and for all, but whose contingent nature – that is, that of being a fact and not an essence of a thing – opens the cogito to the occasion of an infinite repetition, in both its restricted and special extended senses that Sartre now gives to it. This event must take place incessantly and thus is the origin of temporalisation both in the interiority of the subject and in the Other. 'It [the apodictic event, or the event of apodicticity] is as a prehistoric temporalization of simultaneity that we shall consider it here . . . It is as fact – as a primary and perpetual fact – not an essential necessity that we shall study being-for-others' (BN: 377).

As I have already indicated above, it is precisely at this point in the analytic of the Other that Sartre abruptly interrupts his meditation on the history of the concept and goes outside to sit in a public park. So we will follow him. What does he experience if not what he has just described as the apodictic existence of another person who suddenly appears in his perceptual field as a contingent but necessary fact? 'I am in a public park. Not far away there is a lawn and along the edge of that lawn, there are benches. A man passes by those benches' (BN: 341). In other words, at this moment we are returned to a position of 'natural consciousness', rather than the abstract subject of the cogito. We are in the world, and there I catch sight of another person who is in the world too, a real other person and not just a concept, or a mental image, a projection of cogito 'reflecting its own matter' in the form of thought. How refreshing after all that mental labour of the previous analytical work! how courteous and thoughtful for Sartre to take us out for a walk like a dog in the park! In order to savour this moment, therefore, I will recount it in detail:

> I am in a public park. Not far away there is a lawn and along the edge of the lawn there are benches.
> [. . .]
> A man passes by those benches. I see this man.
> [. . .]
> If I were to think of him as a puppet, I should only apply to him the catego-ries I ordinary use to group temporal-spatial 'things'. . . . His relation with other objects would be of a purely additive type; this means that I could have him disappear without the relations of the other objects around him being perceptibly changed.
> [. . .]
> Perceiving him as a man, on the other hand, is not to apprehend an additive relation between the chair and him; it is to register an organization without distance of things in my universe around a privileged object. . . . Instead of the two terms of the distance [i.e., the lawn and the chair, or bench] being indifferent, the distance is unfolded starting from the man whom I see and extending up to the lawn as the synthetic upsurge of a univocal relation. We are dealing with a relation without parts, given at one stroke, in side of which

there unfolds a spatiality which is not my spatiality; for instead of a grouping toward me of objects, there is now an orientation which flees from me.
[. . .]
To the extent that the man-as-object is a fundamental term of this relation, to the extent that this relation reaches toward him, it escapes me. I cannot put myself at the center of it. . . . It stands as a background of things, a background which on principle escapes me and which is conferred on them from without.
[. . .]
The Other is first a permanent flight of things toward a goal which I apprehend as an object at a certain distance from me but which escapes me inasmuch as it unfolds about itself its own distances.
[. . .]
But the Other is still an object for me. He belongs to my distances; . . . hence the disintegration of the universe is contained within the limits of the same universe; we are not dealing here with a flight of the world toward nothingness or outside itself. Rather it appears that the world has a kind of drain hole in the middle of its being and that it is perpetually flowing off through this hole.
[. . .]
(BN: 341–4)

It is in the last description that we now have a better sense of what was early called a 'primary and perpetual fact' of the Other as a drain hole or a singularity that threatens to suck everything into its universe. The Other is a universe that is stuck into the middle of my universe; however, it is only the *fact* that the Other is also – that is, simultaneously – an object that appears to be part of my perceptual field that a safety barrier is installed that, like a damn, prevents my universe from being completely drained off in the instant of the encounter. Nevertheless, as Sartre adds, there still remains a kind of slow leaking of my universe through the drain in the being of the Other, and this slow leak can be identified with the effect of a 'pre-historic temporalization'. It is clear that it is from this description that Deleuze will derive a major component of his own concept of the other person as an expression of the possible world, the imbrication of one perceptual field within a multiplicity of others, which 'leads us to consider the components of this field for itself in a new way' (WP: 18). In short, the other person, which in Sartre's description appears as a 'privileged object', for Deleuze becomes the condition under which 'not only the subject and object are redistributed but also figure and ground, margins and center, moving object and reference point, transitive and substantial, length and depth' (WP: 18).

Earlier in *Difference and Repetition*, Deleuze defines this condition following Leibniz as a 'center of envelopment' (i.e., a monad), and in this way we can also understand Sartre's definition of 'an organization without distance of things in my universe around a privileged object' as also monadic. An organisation of things in my universe, yet without distance, is another way of expressing an enveloping interiority of another spatiality within my perceptual field, meaning that it is without extension and does not belong to the same exteriority as objects. At the same time, this interiority does not correspond to the interiority of the subject either, who is excluded and thus 'without doors or windows', and this gives it the characteristic of an orientation that withdraws, or 'flees from me'. In other words, my spatiality is drained off precisely at the point where another person enters my perceptual field, and flows into an interiority that is defined as being neither nothingness, nor outside of this world, but rather, 'there is a total space which is grouped around the Other, and moreover, this space is made with my space' (BN: 343). Again, as Sartre writes, 'The Other person is that object in the world that determines an internal flow of the universe, an internal hemorrhage' (BN: 345).

Secondly, if we have identified the primary component of Deleuze's concept from the analysis of Sartre, which in turn is derived from a common source in Leibniz, what about the second component: the look? For Sartre, as we know, it is the presence of the look that is deduced from the expression of the other person in my perceptual field; moreover, it is the concrete term that forms the fundamental connection between the self and Other. 'At each instant the Other is looking at me', and it is on the condition of this perpetual gaze that I am for the Other (BN: 345). How is this so and why? In Sartre the subject is described as a constant flight towards objectivity, which represents precisely a freedom from interiority, which the subject seeks to escape through an incessant striving for the peaceful world of objects (in a manner that prefigures the ego appearance as an object among other objects in Lacan's description of the mirror phase). This description of the subject will be no different from what we found in Kant, where the condition of objectivity in general is required for there to be a subject, except here we have the expression of a desire to flee, to escape precisely by fleeing towards the world of objects in order to be 'absorbed' in them. And yet, something happens in the course of this flight: suddenly there is the appearance of an object that withdraws or withholds itself from the subject's flight into exteriority, and moreover, the implication of another interiority that is deeper and more terrifying than my own, given that it is closed, having neither doors nor windows. For Sartre, it is the look that constitutes the event of this sudden revelation; and for Deleuze, it is the sudden appearance of a 'frightened face'. Here, we find the second component in both theories of the Other, which are consequently the same: the 'look' in Sartre = 'the frightened face' in Deleuze.

But why is fear presented as a dominant mood? And in what sense can a frightened face necessarily be compared to what appears in Sartre's analysis of the look? Of course, in Sartre, we also find the expression of fear, but this refers to the subject's initial state of anticipation that causes it to flee through transcendence into the world of objects; that is, to escape its initial state of insecurity and terror precisely through a knowledge of objects, and of the world. Fear, therefore, defines the initial state of being and the consequent desire for transcendence over this being primarily through knowledge of objects. In other words, fear is equal to the cause of desire for transcendence, as well as the primary motive for objective knowledge of the ego itself, which is reduced to the status of being a peculiar object among other objects. As I have already noted, in Kant, it is this equation of fear = desire for transcendence that is missing, except in the instance of the apprehension of a sublime object, which leads Kant to directly identify transcendence with the overpowering nature of reason itself. By contrast, Sartre's analysis is much more mundane in that the desire for transcendence does not lead us to the apprehension of a sublime object, but rather simply to the look of another person who looks at me, of something that escapes me and 'steals away with the world', and at the same time becomes present as an object in my perceptual field. In other words, we do not need any mountains or stormy oceans to present a situation where the faculty of the imagination fails to synthesise an object for the understanding; we simply need another person to look at us, that is to say, the sublimity of a face in my perceptual field. The face is equal to the look in the sense that it appears in front of the eyes, which are objects in the world, *partes extra partes*, but it is only the face that surges in front of the eyes and expresses a sense of an orientation of my attention to a point that withdraws from my consciousness of objects.

According to this simple fable, the ego seeks to escape from the uncertainty of its being by first directing all of its attention on the objects of the external world in order to transcend this state of uncertainty, the being of the 'I am' that bears no other objective form than mere factual existence that remains for myself (i.e., pure inwardness); in its flight towards the world of objects it suddenly encounters in the visage of another person, an image of its own desire reflected in an object that stares back. It is recoiled by this look, which suddenly converts the desire for transcendence into a form of immanence – that is to say, the encounter of two desires that suddenly confronting one another in a field of immanent probabilities, as when Hegel says in the first pages of *The Phenomenology of Spirit* that consciousness is composed of two unequal desires that must be mediated by a third term. For Sartre, fear raises in the ego the object-cause of its desire to look outside itself in the first place, or to the out of field, which is the gesture of turning away from and the inability to see itself. It is already in the movement of turning away from my own being, as from the horror that this being creates in me, that I turn all my attention onto the world that is populated with objects and others. But at this point the orientation that informs consciousness of the external world and the perception of the objects that this world contains is suddenly coupled with the initial fear of the being that 'I am', that is the interiority of an impersonal self whose matter is unformed and chaotic. In short, the very desire to see (= the world) is coupled with an equal, if not greater, desire NOT to look (= at myself). Thus, neither consciousness nor perception are neutral to the compulsion of desire, and there is no objectivity that is not already conditioned by the desire to NOT to look, to flee the self and go unconscious by becoming 'a subject who regards objects', rather than a subject who regards itself, or rather, a subject who thinks myself alone.

For Sartre, it is the Other's look that reflects the movement of transcendence, causing it to turn inwards again, but this time to flow towards a point that 'flees from me', in the sense that the look is the revelation of an object that turns its face away from me at the very moment that it looks at me. It is in this last sense that I think we have a pretty good characterisation of the face of the other person as a strange object whose very manner of appearing is turning away from the subject. Following Sartre's analysis closely at this point, it is this very aspect of turning away and of an interiority that is without distance that causes the ego to 'go towards the others' even more desperately than before, with even greater fear and uncertainty, with an even greater desire for transcendence (i.e., the power of negation to subsume the object in the immanent movement of consciousness); only this time, it is not only the fear of itself that causes this desire, but the fear of the interiority of the Other, that is expressed by the Other and by others, that causes the ego to flee towards the other precisely in an effort to convert immanence into transcendence. Here, in other words, the desire for transcendence is not interrupted, but is simply extended now to include the Other. It is in this sense that we have Sartre's partial solution to the problem of solipsism in the concept of the other person, the ego can only go encounter the Other in its own movement of transcendence towards the objectification of its being as an object of consciousness, but the more it seeks to flee its own certainty through the objectification of the other, the more this object looks away, or turns its back on this desire, as if it barely concerned the ego and remains indifferent to its desire.

For Deleuze, on the other hand, the problem of solipsism is not the problem he is seeking to resolve with his concept of the other person, nor is the problem of the ethical relation with others (or the Absolute Other), as it was for Levinas. It is simply for this reason that he will take the components that he needs from Sartre's analysis, but as if to arrange them in a completely different manner, and according to the requirements of a different problem, in the creation (or re-creation) of the concept. In *Difference and Repetition*, the problem is expressed in terms of the need for centres of envelopment within psychic systems to 'testify to the presence of individuating factors' in these systems. Here, others are simply the name for these centres of envelopment, which are then individuated in the form of the other subject and the self. Once again, here I would say that Deleuze is merely echoing Leibniz's theory of monads as 'simple substances', according to the same requirement that there be centres of envelopment operating in any psychic system, that is, in any living organisation. Moreover, as is also the case with Leibniz, monads are not likened or derived from the empirical ego or conscious reflection of global persons (or subjects), but can also appear as what Deleuze and Guattari call 'larval subjects' that exist in any psychic system as the cause of individuation. Thus, as Deleuze writes, in a purely Leibnizian manner, 'if an organism may be regarded as a microscopic being, how much more is this true of the Other in Psychic systems?' (DR: 261). Accordingly, others are also these larval subjects, or these microscopic beings, that operate in my perceptual field and cause it to undergo modification and change. 'It presents only events, that is, possible worlds as concepts, and other people as expressions of possible worlds or conceptual personae' (WP: 47–8). The flux of events that constitute a perceptual field are not immanent to an individualised form that belongs to a self or a subject. In fact, one does not even require the form of the subject to constitute the perceptual field, since the perceptual field is related to the plane of immanence described as an immanent survey (*survol*) of a field without subject; 'the Other person does not restore transcendence to another self but returns every other self to the immanence of the field surveyed' (WP: 47). Consequently, as Deleuze will say of Husserl and all the phenomenology that followed, it installed the mole of transcendence in hiding in the immanence of the Flesh, that is, in the absolute limit of consciousness in creating a 'fetish' of the Other's body. By contrast, in extending the cogito to the form of the Other, Sartre does not fetishise the Other's difference but restores it to the same form of immanence as the cogito itself – facticity or apodictic existence – thus 'his presupposition of an impersonal transcendental field', as Deleuze says, 'restores the rights of immanence' to the cogito (WP: 47).

It is actually Gilbert Simondon who already solves this problem and provides Deleuze with the necessary 'bridge', so to speak, that will also lead to a revision of the concept of the category itself as a principle of ontogenesis rather than a metaphysical principle which radically transforms the a priori character that is identified with the concept of the Other. In fact, I would suggest that Simondon's success in solving the problem of passing from the plane of constituted individuation to what Deleuze will henceforth call, following Simondon, 'pre-individual reality' cannot be overstated and even constitutes something of a critical turning point in Deleuze's philosophy. In many respects, Deleuze's concept of the Other can simply be clarified, following Simondon, as a new principle of individuation that does not have the constituted unity of individual as the first term, whether we are speaking of the subject of the perceptual field, or the subject of consciousness, as a principle or first term in the ontogenesis of the ego. In other words, this first term must be subtracted as a principle in any construction of the ontogenesis of the psychic system – as one could argue both Sartre and Simondon have both done using very different methods – in order to rectify the real character of individuation itself as a becoming rather than referring to any already constituted term or principle of identity, or, as Simondon says, 'to begin by placing the constituted individual into a system of reality'. For both Deleuze and Simondon, therefore, the problem lies with previous theories of individuation which take the subject as the first principle, in an axiomatic or categorical manner. For example, from the revised introduction that appears in the 1989 *L'Individuation psychique et collective*, Simondon argues:

> Such a research perspective gives an ontological privilege to the constituted individual. It therefore runs the risk of not producing a true ontogenesis – that is, of not placing the individual into the system of reality in which the individuation occurs. What is postulated in the search for the principle of individuation is that the individuation has a principle. The notion of a principle of individuation arises, in a way, from a genesis in the other direction, a reversed ontogenesis: in order to account for the genesis of the individual with its definitive characteristics, one must suppose the existence of a first term, the principle, which contains that which will explain why the individual is an individual, and which will account for its ecceity. However, it would remain to be shown that the ontogenesis could have a first term as its first condition: a term is already an individual, or, in any case, something individualizable and that can be a source of ecceity and can turn itself into multiple ecceities.[1]

In order to resolve this problem, Simondon reverses the order of the principle of ontogenesis in individuation, and at the same time redefines the sense of the principle itself which Deleuze applies to the concept of category in classical philosophy, which I have discussed earlier on. His application of Simondon is most evident in his reconstruction of the concept of the other person (*autrui*) in which the subject is no longer the first term, or functions as the principle of individuation, but rather the 'Other'. But at this point, however, the term of the 'Other' cannot be identified with another subject, since the principle of individuation that determines a subject is not yet given.

Quoting the original statement from Simondon, which Deleuze actually takes up and applies as a rule in his construction of the concept of the Other in the perceptual field, 'One must begin with individuation, with being grasped at its center according to spatiality and becoming, not with an individual that is substantialized in front of a world that is foreign to it.'[2] To illustrate this, let's return one last time to the concluding pages of *Difference and Repetition* to see how Deleuze applies this very same principle of ontogenesis to the concept of the Other, which actually now represents the 'individuating difference' in psychic systems:

There must none the less be values of implication in psychic systems in the process of being explicated; in other words, there must be centres of envelopment which testify to the presence of individuating factors. These centres are clearly constituted neither by the I nor by the self, but by a completely different structure belonging to the I–Self system. This structure should be designated by the name 'other'. It refers only to the self for the other I and the other I for the self. Theories tend to oscillate mistakenly and ceaselessly from a pole at which the other is reduced to the status of object to a pole at which it assumes the status of subject. Even Sartre was content to inscribe this oscillation in the other as such, in showing that the other became object when I became subject, and did not become subject unless I in turn became object. As a result, the structure of the other, as well as its role in psychic systems, remained misunderstood. The other who is nobody, but who is self for the other and the other for the self in two systems, the a priori Other is defined in each system by its expressive value – in other words, its implicit and enveloping value. (DR: 261–2)

In other words, Deleuze defines the Other as the expression of a value of implication that is present in any psychic system, according to the analogy of how implication function in any living system as the very creative presence of 'life' that resists increasing entropy.

These centres are not the intensive individuating factors themselves, but they are their representatives within a complex whole in the process of explication. It is these which constitute the little islands and the local increases of entropy at the heart of systems which nevertheless conform overall to the principle of degradation: atoms taken individually, for example, even though they none the less confirm the law of increasing entropy when considered en masse in the order of explication of the system in which they are implicated. (DR: 256)

In commenting on these passages, it is important to understand that, contrary to Levinas, Deleuze does not identify the Other itself as the expression of alterity (infinity as the expression of difference and the difference of difference in the psychic system) in the psychic system composed of the I–Self. Rather, he qualifies this identification, as in the above passage, by distinguishing what he calls 'centres of implication or envelopment' (which we could also properly call monads) from 'individuating factors themselves'. Consequently, the 'other' is only a term that represents the presence of this individuating factor in the psychic system, but which actually refers to another psychic system co-implicated with the constituted that operates according to a differentiation pattern, as I will return to explain further on. In other words, as a term, the 'other' is not to be identified with the source of alterity, which means the cause of the real difference between the two psychic systems each of which are co-implicated in the other, and which is here clarified to mean the source of individuation, but rather only with a signifying value that represents the existence of this factor in the psychic system. 'The individual thus finds itself attached to a pre-individual half which is not the impersonal within it so much as the reservoir of its singularities' (DR: 246).

Thus, the term 'Other' in Deleuze's philosophy at this point, rather than standing for the supposed unity and transcendence of the other individual, only functions formally as a term that represents the a priori nature of the difference between two psychic systems and consequently their primordial and pre-individual relation, which appears as a 'sign' or a 'symbol' – however, contrary to the Greek sense, the two halves that exist, yet as broken pieces that do belong to a former totality, but as being 'unequal in themselves'. Moreover, each piece of the symbol of the I and Self becomes greater or lesser in proportion depending on which perspective or point of view that one assumes in the total psychic system. It is this mobile perspective that accounts for both the possible of the function of the shifter in language systems and also the two poles that belong to the image in the system of consciousness, which constitutes the objective and subjective halves that enter into what Deleuze critiques as a 'strange oscillation' between subject and object poles. In his construction of the concept of the other person (*autrui*), both in *Difference and Repetition* and also cited again at the beginning of *What is Philosophy?* It is the primary nature of this 'sign' that is constituted by what is essentially a philosophy of the fragment, following Blanchot, that the fragmentary sign that represents the coupling of the constituted individual and pre-individual reality is further represented by a face that expresses this differential factor in psychic experience and in language, or a few words, that actualise this difference within consciousness. I will simply note here that the objective and subjective poles have now been replaced by a partial image (partial because its other half refers to a place out of field or out of frame, as in cinema, as in the case of the terrified face) and the expression of a phrase, or language fragment (fragmentary because only expression is required to actualise and does not require sense of a complete phrase, or even sense defined by logical propositions, as in the statement from *Logical Investigations*, 'I have an unconscious toothache').

Second, it is important to underline the fact that Deleuze strongly distinguishes the forms of the I and the self from the Other as a 'centre of envelopment' or as the term that 'expresses the value of implication' in the psychic system.

> The individuating factors or the implicated factors of individuation therefore have neither the form of the I nor the matter of the Self. This is because the I is inseparable from a form of identity, while the Self is indistinguishable from a matter constituted by a continuity of resemblances. The differences included within the I and the Self are, without doubt, borne by individuals: nevertheless, they are not individual or individuating to the extent that they are understood in relation to this identity in the I and this resemblance in the Self. By contrast, every individuating factor is already difference and difference of difference. (DR: 257)

In the above statements, Deleuze merely deduces the existence of the 'Other Structure' from the fact that neither the I nor the self can be said to function as individuating factors in the psychic system, since they already appear as expressing the form/matter distinction of the psychic system. The I is the universal form of the psychic system; the self is the indeterminate matter of any psychic system. In other words, they are the expressed values of an already constituted psychic system and the values they express are already internal to the system and testify to its functioning according to differences that are already established. As Deleuze writes, 'The I therefore appears at the end as the universal form of psychic life, just as the Self is the universal matter of that form. The I and the Self explicate one another, and do so endlessly throughout the entire history of the Cogito' (DR: 257). It is from this that Deleuze deduces another system within the system of the I–Self, a system within the system, co-implicated within the psychic structure constituted by the I and the self, and assigns this other system the real function of what he calls a 'individuating factor', the expression of real 'difference and difference of difference' – that is, a system of alterity, or what he refers to at this early point, an 'Other Structure'.

Since I have come to the end of my exposition of the concept of 'another person' (and I am quite exhausted without, however, completely exhausting the problem), I cannot develop in detail the implication of Deleuze's choice of the term 'Structure' to represent this second psychic system implicated in the psychic system of the I–Self. Suffice it to say that this corresponds to Deleuze's definition of any structure as two series that are linked by a third term that functions as signifying element in both series, and in this case this corresponds to the term 'Other' that Deleuze employs to represent – and this is his word – a factor of individuation as well as a term that actually belongs to the field already constituted by individuals, thus linking the appearance of every Other in the psychic system of the cogito a 'pre-individual reality'. Here we find a precise definition of *autrui* as 'a reservoir of singularities' that is coupled with a constituted individual entity, which in many respects both echoes Sartre's first definition of the pure cogito as an impersonal transcendental field that is purified of any *egology*. However, here even the character of the purity or impersonal is redefined in order to avoid the association with the phenomenological reduction of consciousness; consequently, the Other expresses the character of individuation that does not have the individual as the first term, or the initial state, but rather is the pre-individual half that is always coupled with the individual and opens it to all other possible states and intentions, according to a beautiful description from Simondon's *L'Individuation psychique et collective* that informs Deleuze and Guattari's later works concerning the principle of individuation that belongs to any assemblage:

The psycho-social world of the transindividual is neither purely social nor the interindividual; it supposes a veritable operation of individuation from the basis of a preindividual reality, linked to the individuals and capable of constituting a new problematic with its own metastability. It expresses a quantum condition, correlative to a plurality of orders of magnitude. The living is presented as a problematic being that is at the same time superior and inferior to unity. To say that the living being is problematic is to consider becoming as a dimension of the living: the living is according to its becoming, which operates a mediation. The living is both agent and theater of individuation; its becoming is a permanent individuation, or rather, a series of outbreaks of individuation advancing from one metastability to another. The individual is thus neither substance nor a simple part of the collective: the collective intervenes as a resolution of the individual problematic, which means that the basis of the collective reality is already partially contained in the individual, in the form of the preindividual reality that remains linked to the individuated reality; that which we generally consider to be a relation, because of the mistaken hypothesis of the substantialization of individual reality, is in fact a dimension of the individuation through which the individual becomes. The relation – to the world and to the collective – is a dimension of individuation in which the individual participates starting from the preindividual reality that individuates itself step by step.[3]

To conclude my exposition or pedagogy of the concept of *autrui*, I have tried to demonstrate the 'problem solving' character of the process Deleuze describes as the creation of concepts (i.e., philosophical constructivism). At the same time, I do not believe that Deleuze introduces anything new than what Sartre has already provided him for the concept of the Other person. Rather, he has merely rearranged the different components of Sartre's more original concept, highlighting or producing different features from these 'components' (as he later calls them in *What is Philosophy?*), and reorganising them to function in a different manner so that the Other comes first, that is, prior to the subject. In other words, Deleuze did not invent the concept of the other person, Sartre did; but even before Sartre there was Leibniz. Deleuze only improves the concept, which he found unsatisfactory for reasons that I have already explained, by subtracting one of its major parts, or at least by minimising its role in the new assemblage. But then, isn't this how philosophy always progresses through the creation of new concepts; not a creation ex nihilo, but a refabricating of bits and pieces derived from previous concepts, and getting them to work in a new order, and in order to produce different effects? I would even argue that Deleuze's concept does not necessary represent a progress over the previous one, or that he radically departs from Sartre's concept of 'the Other', but rather only that he restores an earlier arrangement of the impersonal transcendental field that he originally found in *Transcendence of the Ego*, especially given the fact that he thinks Sartre made a mistake a few years later in *Being and Nothingness* by putting so much emphasis on the 'look' in the analytic of the existence of others, which created a mysterious and unlocalisable oscillation between components, and, even worse, risked reintroducing a subject–object duality – if not the subject itself – back into this field and thus destroying the possibilities of pure immanence. So much for the history of philosophy, and as he states many times, concepts can be badly botched and problems badly posed (for example, the problem of solipsism in Sartre). Of course, since we are speaking of a 'history' and not a metaphysical state of affairs, this state is not permanent, even though Deleuze admits that some bad concepts have lasted a long time, since concepts can always be re-created by simply rearranging their components. Consequently, if there is one overriding message that is expressed throughout Deleuze and Guattari's last work, *What is Philosophy?*, it is the complete liberation of the practical creation of concepts according to problems from the straitjacket of the history of philosophy, but especially from its Heideggerian and Derridean versions of 'the End of Metaphysics'. In response, they say: 'If you don't like a concept (e.g., the Subject, History, the One, Being, etc.), then simply create a new one in its place, but under the provision that whatever concept you create must actually work, and with the knowledge that you never convince anyone. Perhaps even more than religion, philosophy is a cult that is actually much more severe in granting immortality to those who believe in it. As Deleuze says somewhere in *Bergsonism*, there are still only a finite number of Great Souls that seem to speak with one another across vast deserts of philosophical duration. Even today, every philosopher craves immortality. Deleuze's reply would be a bit like the Gospel of James: it is by works and not by faith that one is given immortality; moreover, it is by becoming impersonal, a conceptual persona like 'the Christ', that something like immortality is actually given. As for the individual philosopher, there is only death.

Notes

1. Simondon, L'Individuation psychique et collective, pp. 8–9.
2. Ibid., p. 8.
3. Ibid., pp. 10–11.

5. 'In-Human Sex' ('Desiring-Machines')

In human sexuality, the determination of another person would appear as a means to satisfying a craving or demand that originates in the ego and depends on the other's subordination. The other acquiesces and satisfies an aim whose character is as impersonal as it is unconscious, which is to say, unknowable in terms of its own intentionality. Even the act of so-called mutual pleasure betrays the essential impersonality of a desire that does not aim to encounter another independent consciousness, but instead slips away to the hither side of consciousness where self and other are two poles mapped onto a body without organs (i.e., a whole that neither totalises nor unifies the parts). In this sense, Levinas was correct in recognising that sensuality and proximity express a passivity that is more passive than consciousness, which turn the ego's own relationship to the other into an obsession.

Following Deleuze and Guattari, perhaps another way of approaching the obsessive and impersonal character of desire is to recognise in its nature something that is fundamentally machinic, which opens a dimension of what Deleuze calls 'the non-human sex' in humankind. In a short review on Pierre Bénichou's study of masochism from the early 1970s, Deleuze writes:

> Your particular desiring-machines: what are they? In a difficult and beautiful text, Marx called for the necessity to think human sexuality not only as a relation between human sexes, masculine and feminine, but as a relation between 'the human sex and the non-human sex'. He was clearly not thinking of animals, but of what is non-human in human sexuality: the machines of desire. (DI: 243)

What, then, does Deleuze mean when he names the 'other sex', not in anthropomorphic terms, but following Marx, as the otherness of sexuality itself, as the non-human within human sexuality?

In pursuing this reference by Deleuze to Marx's 1843 *Critique of Hegel's Philosophy of Right*, where the statement concerning the difference between 'the human sex and the non-human sex' supposedly appears, I will briefly turn to a series of lectures that no doubt Deleuze and Guattari were familiar with in the early 1970s when they conceived of the desiring machine: Althusser's series of lectures later published in 1978 under the title *Marx dans ses limites*. There we have a striking discussion from a treatise of Lenin on the state as a 'machine unlike any other social apparatus or assemblage'. Consequently, the state is distinguished from any number of other social forms found in the sphere of civil society: the association, the counsel, the league, the organization, the political party, the church, nor even the 'organism'. According to Lenin, this is what makes the state special, and for Althusser (as for Marx) this would mean that it is composed of a special kind of material. Thus, 'the State is a special machine in the sense that it is made of another metal . . ., another *"matière"*, which has a completely different consistency'.[1] Here we might ask, 'A different consistency than what?', and here we are referred back to the previous social organisations of civil society, which are composed from the ideological forms of interest. In fact, they are the materialisation and embodiment of these interests in corporate life, or, as Hegel said, in 'ethical life'.

As with any machine, in inquiring after how it works, the very first question one must ask is where does it derive its energy to function in the first place. This is because all machines are, by their very nature, 'mechanical'. Interestingly, this fact is why Althusser understands Marx's rejection of the term 'organism' to refer to the state, and, by extension, why I would also understand Deleuze and Guattari to never use the term 'organism' to apply to desire, since even though desire includes organisms and organic or sexual components, including individual bodies, its nature is purely machinic in determining how these individuals and sexual components are included in the whole, how they function together in a unity, towards a prospective goal. But what is even more surprising is that after the nineteenth century the term 'mechanical' itself can no longer serve to define the term 'machine'. This is because the organic is already a metaphor of mechanism, applied to nineteenth-century biology, and thus the mechanical teleology, which stems from the even earlier, Aristotelian understanding of nature, cannot serve as the ground for understanding the modern machine. Thus, the special

machine of the state cannot be described from the principles that belong
to the general field of mechanics.

In the section of *Das Kapital* on the question of surplus value, it is
here (according to Althusser) that Marx gives us an indication of the
special machine he has in mind by quoting the following definition
from Charles Babbage: 'a machine is formed by the reunion of all these
simple instruments that are placed in motion by a unique motor'.[2] It is
here that Marx understands the special nature of a machine, opposed
to a simple mechanical apparatus, by the uniqueness of the motor than
causes all the components to move together, by the nature of the force
that causes them to move. For example, Marx writes, 'the infant has
his own force of movement just as the steam engine', and the function
of the motor that is special to each kind of machine is described as the
transformation of one kind of energy into another (for example, caloric
energy into kinetic energy).[3]

By means of this specific definition, Marx is able to determine the
'special machine' of the state by the uniqueness of its motor from
which it derives its energy to function: the transformation of the energy
released by class inequality into the energy that drives the state through
legal violence. The law is a force that functions as the motor of the state
and in which all individuals recognise it as a special kind of machine
that appears from the 'outside' and functions automatically; however,
the machine derives its energy by converting raw class inequality into
legal violence by which the state first appears to separate itself from civil
society only to more effectively intervene into corporate life, including
the life of the family, and to enforce its own form of universal right. It is
only in this way that we can understand how the reproduction of class
inequality, even the production of new forms of inequality, provides
the motor of the state-machine with the energy it needs to function.
Although it seems that the state exists to end these forms of inequality,
this is ideology *tout court!* Simply put, new forms of inequality provide
the state-machine with the energy it requires to function and to expand
across the entire *socius*; it can even be said to drill into the *socius* to discover new sources of the energy it demands. Finally, it is even this transformation of energy that is responsible for fabrication of the special body
of the state and its functionaries (the police, the military, the bureaucrats,
the corporation), because the very metal of their body and consistency
from which it is composed is suddenly transformed into a unified and
special matter in the same way that the bodies of soldiers in a platoon

have the consistency of one kind of metal, or bureaucrats in a vast office in Kafka can be said to all be materially *made from the same cloth.* Likewise, we could say that the material that the desiring-machine is made from – and here I am referring neither to the biological substrate nor to the symbolic distinction between the sexes – is composed of two distinctive materials, or *matières,* the human sex and the non-human sex.

It is from this last observation that I will now return to Deleuze and Guattari's concept of the desiring-machine in order to ask in what way it fabricates a special body, or that each sexuality might be better understood (no longer in analogy to the biological determination of different species-beings, as still in the case of psychoanalytic description of perversions) as made up of another *matière,* sexuality being understood only as a certain kind of matter that is produced by a very particular (or special) set of desiring-machines. We can argue that the same determination of the machine, or, if you would prefer employing the old language, 'materialist determination' can be applied to determine the special nature of the desiring-machine in Deleuze and Guattari's theory. According to Deleuze, what is remarkable of the 'non-human sex' is a function, or a set of functions, that appear only evident, for example, in real masochism or schizophrenia. What is particularly revealing about this 'functionalism' is that it reduces the concrete individuals to abstractions that serve the impersonal or non-human goals of particular desiring-machines. When we speak of real masochism, for example, we are referring to this impersonal element of desire at the basis of most particular masochisms, which is not understood in terms of a structure. Rather, this impersonal element refers to its function, its manner of functioning, how it works. In explaining this function, following Deleuze and Guattari, we do not resort to the notion of a structure, which would unify all the component parts as terms of signification in a unifying sense. Desire does not function in this way; it simply works (or does not work, which means that even in not working it functions in a particular way). Its terms are purely machinic. Only psychoanalysis seeks to give desire a meaning – even that of a general structure or ontological horizon of sense – within the field of human sexuality.

Very early on, Deleuze was interested in an analysis of sexuality that was purely functional, premised on the production of 'real desiring-machines'; thus, masochism was viewed from the perspective of the particular kind of desiring-machine it produces in relation to the big social and technological machines. Later, with Guattari, he goes on to explore other kinds of desiring-machines providing that they were also real (real paranoid machines, real schizophrenic machines, etc.) and not reduced to psychoanalytic interpretation. Certainly, the 'non-human sex' in sexuality can be recognised as its tendency to function more or less impersonally in combining bodies, statements, feelings, even qualities of pleasure and pain, into an assemblage that 'works' by determining the prevalence of certain desiring-machines that function socially and politically as well. What Deleuze and Guattari call 'Oedipus' is just one desiring-machine among others; consequently, the question of ethics in Deleuze and Guattari's work becomes the following: 'What are your special desiring-machines? How do they work?'

We can see the clear parallel with Marx's approach above; in responding to the question 'What is the state?' Marx only asked how it worked, what it does, what it produced – because he already understood its entire meaning was bound up with its function. He already knew it was a special kind of machine; therefore, in asking questions about machines, form follows function. In asking the question 'What is a nuclear particle accelerator?' this is not an ontological question. One might also compare this to Kafka's approach in 'In the Penal Colony' when, in reply to the question 'What is the Law?', we have an intricate description of an apparatus, its gears and levers, its harness and straps, the way the victim is placed, the method of inscription, and so on. Deleuze and Guattari approach the question of human sexuality in the same way – how does it work, what are its parts, how do they come together into an assemblage, what do they produce? And presuming there is more than one organisation of human sexuality – but this is already an empirical observation, and not a moral judgement – the question becomes how desire functions. In other words, what are the particular desiring-machines that make up the field of human sexuality. Psychoanalysis, according to the critique of Deleuze and Guattari, which in an important way parallels the earlier critique of Marx against Hegel, 'anthropomorphizes the entire field of sexuality' in the same way that Hegel ideologises the theory of the state. Human sexuality does not emerge from the principle of the organism, but is made from an entirely special matter, which has its own consistency and composition. By contrast, Deleuze and Guattari do not anthropomorphise sexuality, which means that they do not leave it a mystery; if it is unconscious, it is only because this refers to the machinic element of desire, the 'non-human sex in sexuality', which is only a mystery from the perspective of *how it really works*.

Let us take as an example the simplest of machines, the one that Deleuze and Guattari often resort to in their analysis to provide an analysis: 'the sucking-machine'. This is differentiated from the organ of the mouth, which is also defined by machines that flow (spitting, vomiting, speaking, etc.) and each of these could be said to be desiring-machines as well depending on the assemblages they belong to. When coupled to another machine defined by a flow (the breast-machine, for example) it can be described as an intricate mechanism of organs (lips, teeth, tongue, larynx or throat) that all function together to produce a flow through a series of breaks or cuts; in other words, the machine is described as a concert of intricate functions that are given a goal: to suck. This series of actions takes place through disjunctions, or, as Deleuze and Guattari define, *prélèvements de flux*, in this case, by a series of gulps performed when the lips close off a flow and cut off a morsel or portion, and the throat detaches the morsel through the larynx and into the stomach. Deleuze and Guattari describe this entire process of *prélèvements de flux* as what happens when a slicing-machine cuts portions from the thigh of a pig. Later on, these morsels that are detached from the flow come to acquire their own meaning as partial objects that are internalised in the body and can be determined as either good or bad – milk, sperm, urine, vaginal discharge, shit – and even involving a reactive counter-flux such as vomiting or spitting out.

If the mouth will become a privileged organ, it is only because it exists at the intersection or along the crack that runs between the body and the brain, one that precedes the eye, whose later supremacy could be understood as being bound up with the apparatus of recording. In fact, humanity can be defined as a species that relates to its immediate environment in a peculiar manner – by sticking everything in its mouth in order to place objects derived from the external world into contact with the brain. Sooner or later, everything ends up there, including the world itself. This presupposes that the mouth functions as a special motor that determines the production of the desiring-machines, a motor that functions by detaching and by slicing off, by including what is detached, and by partitioning what is continuous (in breathing, for example, which portions out a continuous flow of air), by what Deleuze and Guattari define as disjunctive and connective syntheses. The baby from the first moment of its awakening life relates everything through its mouth, but it is the particular mistake of psychoanalysis to map this relation back onto the different parts of its parents' bodies, and to make it derive from

Global Persons. 'Strictly speaking', they write, 'it is not true that a baby experiences his mother's breast as a separate part of her body. It exists, rather, as part of a desiring-machine connected to the baby's mouth' (AO: 201).

On the other hand, what is the reality of the child in the first days of life? What are his or her real desiring-machines, recalling the original hermaphroditic organisation of the sexes, before they have been 'cut off' and separated out by language – so the pronominal distinction between gender would not even make sense here. As in the case of Proust, as Deleuze discovered, 'in the mystery of an initial hermaphroditism . . . the vegetal theme takes on its full significance, in opposition to the *logos-as-organism*: hermaphroditism is not the property of a now lost animal totality, but the actual partitioning of the two sexes in one and the same plant' (P: 135). Thus, the child is not asexual but, as Freud had already intuited, polysexual, or polymorphously perverse, which is to say, capable of entertaining relation to the sexes, and these would certainly amount to more than two, since the child is also capable of emulating the sexual characteristic of plants and animals, but equally importantly – and this constitutes Deleuze and Guattari's greatest insight following the work of Klein, Bettelheim and Jung (and not Freud), but also of Proust, Beckett and Artaud – the sexuality of machines as well. For example, they write 'let us consider the child at play, or a child crawling about and exploring the various rooms in the house where he lives, looking intensely at an electrical outlet . . .' (AO: 46).

It is not by accident then that Deleuze and Guattari seek to discover the positive reality of the child's relation to the world of partial objects, and that this relation is primarily defined as machinic, or in purely machinic terms, keeping in mind that certain machines function by exploding as much as organising a flow of energy into a productive continuum. It is also not by accident that Deleuze and Guattari find in certain writers that they choose an intense curiosity with the positive discovery of the power contained in partial objects to reorganise the whole, as if these objects were capable of storing the energy of creation itself. What is Proust's *madeleine*, for example, but a partial object of this type and, moreover, a desiring-machine that is connected by means of the mouth. Although the example of the partial object derived from Beckett, that of Molloy's 'sucking stones', is often cited, it is just as often completely misunderstood. The relation between the sucking stone and the partial object derived from the mother's body is even offered up as a joke at the very beginning of the novel (recalling here that Beckett was analysed by Melanie Klein). The mother's breast is dried up – she is either dead or merely desiccated, only her senile head remains – the sexes have been replaced by a series of more primary couples all of which differ only by a detachment of a chain of associations (Molloy, Malone, Mahood, Moran, etc.). The literary machine often has as its goal the discovery of more primary couples, detached from the parents and even from the sexual couples. Beckett always discovers behind each couple a more primary couple that is non-familial and even non-human.

As Deleuze and Guattari constantly claim, psychoanalysis has botched its understanding of the real transformative role of partial objects by 'mapping them back' onto the Oedipal body without organs; thus, recalling the precise definition of the apparatus given above, Oedipus is an apparatus of recording that provides all the desiring-machines with a unique direction that causes them to function to fabricate a social body that is wedded to the bourgeois order. It is for this reason that Deleuze and Guattari accuse psychoanalysis of 'taking part in the work of bourgeois repression at its most far-reaching level, that is to say, keeping European humanity harnessed to the yoke of daddy-mommy and *making no effort to do away with this problem once and for all*' (AO: 50). Nevertheless, they argue, at some point Oedipus was open to the entire social field, 'to a field of production directly invested by the libido', and the real problem is what happened that caused this form of desiring production to close up, in other words, what made it into an apparatus that caused all desire to flow into such a narrow channel defined by the family and its surrogates, as if to box up the productive relations of desire and to create non-communicating mediations that lead to repression of the positive reality of the desiring-machines.

Let us take as an example the body that usually appears in Oedipal sexuality, belonging to what Deleuze and Guattari call the mommy-daddy-me apparatus? Originally, the organisation of phallic-heterosexuality works by converting the inequality of the sexes into a special body, as well as a legalised form of masculine violence (a sadistic impulse). It is simply the case that we mistake this force as desire, this 'surplus-value' produced by inequality as pleasure. On the other hand, masochism can be defined as a special kind of machine that allows these energies to become perceptible – humiliation, mastery, subordination, subjugation, ownership, usury (or prostitution) – whereas, normative heterosexuality mystifies these inequalities in the form of sexuality itself. Elsewhere I have argued that the nineteenth-century Freud had clearly understood the dominant libidinal organisation as sadistic (meaning, masculine or phallic organisation), which implied the subordination of the sexual object to the aggressive instincts; actually, a denigration of the role of women in becoming both the object and the intrinsic cause of desire (a position bound up with guilt for the loss of the original narcissism, that is, for the absence of the phallus). If this seems cruel, it is because it is made to compensate for an even greater cruelty inflicted on the child by the original phallic mother, who is actually an amalgamation of the partial objects found in both parents' bodies. If the maternal image is purely fictitious and is a phantasy invented by children, first of all, then, it is perhaps the first of all social myths, followed later on by religions. It is here, as Deleuze says, that the phantasm functions as the original beginning in the same way that an effect is substituted for a cause; the phantasm henceforth projects itself across a surface and organises the sexual zones of the body and, at the same time, cause these images to be introjected into real bodies where they will function in concert with partial objects (both good and bad, tokens of pleasure and pain, but also life and death). However, Deleuze reminds us, following Klein, that the phallic organisation was indeed intended to prevent something worse: the anarchic arrangement of the destructive instincts, including the possibility that they would take the body of the child as their object (i.e., the famous rationalisation for the prohibition against incest).

> The phallus, as an image projected on the genital zone, is not at all an aggressive instrument of penetration and eventration. On the contrary, it is an instrument of the surface, meant to *mend* the wounds that the destructive drives, bad internal objects, and the penis of the depths have inflicted on the maternal body, and to reassure the good object, to convince it not to turn its face away. (The processes of 'reparation' on which Melanie Klein insists seem to belong to the constitution of a surface which is itself restorative.) (LS: 201)

It may seem strange to refer to the phallus as the instrument of original reparation, as an instrument of *pacification* (in the strongest sense of the term). The image given above is that of a war waged by the drives that is followed by a general and indefinite term of peace; of course, the terms of this peace are made by the victor, and Oedipal peace here comes off looking a lot like the MacArthur Plan in many respects. Here again, we come back to Deleuze and Guattari's fundamental question: it is true that Oedipus was originally open, in all directions, to a field of production directly invested by libido, so what causes it to close up? Here, we are given the answer: it is the image of the phallus projected across the genital zone that triangulates the reality of the desiring-machines onto the surface of the body determined by Oedipal sexuality. In other words, Oedipus causes the entire field of desiring production to close up around the body that is determined by sexuality, as if desire from that point onwards only concerned sexuality and its various avatars (or, as Freud would define this, the distinction between normal sexuality and its perversions, which occur when the triangulation effected by the projection of the phallus fails to sew things up and the component instincts separate from the body and return to their earlier stages of dis-order and guerrilla warfare). But what is the meaning of the body that is projected across the surface of the erogenous zones, closed off by sexuality? It is a body closed off from the reality of its own desiring-machines. This is why the forms of human sexuality are so much about plugging up every orifice, by giving every partial object (desiring-machine) something to do, by turning all the desiring machines into an orchestra that constantly play nothing but the sad and mournful riff of Oedipal sexuality. Here, we might ask why so much popular music is about fucking, if not a literal transcription of Oedipal music which fills the environment of the *socius* like ambient sound, so, in the end, no one can escape it. It is really quite comic and horrifying at once: from every nook and cranny, every corner, in every elevator, café or bar, in the home or in the office, in the car next to you at the signal, when you go to bed at night and when you wake up, in hallways, on aeroplanes – Oedipal mood music! 'Baby, gotta get me some . . . huh, huh . . . hot, hot, nasty sex!'

The body is closed off from the reality of the desiring-machines, which means in a certain sense that the body is neutralised or, worse, turned into a corpse from the very beginning. It becomes a dummy, a prop or a tool; it becomes sterile and lifeless double, a doll poked and pulled at as in a child's game or in a porno, an object that belongs to a subject according to a legal or moral code, a fragment of language, a pure image. If there is something vulgar in pornography, it is the literal representation of the function of sexual organs determined as partial objects; there is so much production, producing, machines everywhere and every part or aspect of the body becoming machinic. If there is the 'now you see it and now you don't' that seems to determine the object from the scopic drive, then this is simply the machine nature of the image that is attached to the body of the spectator through the eye; however, this machine is immediately related to others that do not exist within the image and constitute its out of field, populated by machines that enlarge and explode, by detonations and sadness. Guattari certainly understood this best when he said that 'the phallus is the symbol of the body cut off from its own machines . . . The phallus heralds the death of desire and its entrance into the sexual organ'. He writes:

> 'You will be a body – *corpse-body* – a cadaver, not a machine.'
> You will be a man or a woman according to the binary symbol: phallus-non phallus.
> This has nothing to do with the supposed 'entrance into the order of the symbolic'. It's the opposite. The phallus heralds an entrance into the division of the sexes (third internal binary relation, limiting the addition of things and sign multiplicativity). *So what remains is the body (my emphasis)*. You are a man-body or a woman-body, or maybe you are both in alternation. You have a common trunk. Production-reproduction man-woman unit. Your ego is: *a body without a machine*. So the phallus opens up the entrance to the ego, to the massive social body; work unit and reproduction unit (male and female). . . . So, return to Freud: there is indeed a genital phase: the phallus doesn't gloss over the series. It characterizes a specific suppressive operation, that of the division of the sexes. The phallus is the prototype of a dualistic break in the division of labor, and nothing more. (AOP: 292)

Consequently, when we speak of the body, in the manner that we usually do, in the manner we have been taught (and not by our parents since they have been taught to speak that way as well), we are speaking of nothing effectively real, something that has no real effective unity, because in fact it has only the reality of an image. This is its precise onto-logical status; body-image is the remainder, what is left over, from the separation effected by the phallic supplement; it is a fragmentary part that thereafter has the function of a whole. As they write: 'To withdraw a part from the whole, to detach, to "have something left over", is to produce, and to carry out real operations of desire in the material world' (AO: 41). Therefore, to say that under this determination of the image, the desiring-machines have been cut off, or the body-as-image is closed to the reality of the desiring machines, is to say that the effective reality of desire and its production continues to operate through the partial objects that do not compose or have the image of the body as their unity. The body is not a whole of which the partial objects would be the parts, even though this is how the partial objects are usually represented according to the image of normative sexuality, but only in the manner of pieces that do not quite fit and are violently jammed into place. This is why the body, as an object of representation, always fails to grasp the reality of all the partial objects that are constantly interrupting and disturbing this image fundamentally. It is this disturbance of the image that still speaks to the existence of the desiring-machines, and to the fact that they are not completely pacified. Of course, real sexual couples know that the Oedipal image of the sexualised body is completely false. Its perfect image is not unified and constantly breaking down. This why there is so much talk in relationships 'about sexuality' that is really about reassembling the pieces to a machine that is breaking down, on the verge of breaking down, in the process of breaking down, if not broken already. In other words, sooner or later, someone is always talking about fixing things, about getting things up and running again, or putting them into a new order that will work better next time. Therefore, the real question becomes why – if so much of the way that we really talk about sexuality grasps its true reality as machinic, as simply a question of arranging one's own special desiring machines so that they work together – is this opposed to the image of sexuality as a pacified whole, as something that is fundamentally non-machinic?

According to Guattari, this is because the phallus actually represents a form of 'machine-alterity', it is 'other than the machine', an image that henceforth becomes equated with the ego as 'a body without a machine . . . [which] henceforth speaks in the name of the most deterritorialized machinic alterity' (AOP: 293). Here, let me return to rephrase the definition of human sexuality I began with: in so-called human sexuality, the determination of the aim originates in the ego in accordance with the satisfaction the death instinct, which demands nothing less than the suppression of the desiring machines in the name of the most deterritorialized machinic alterity. In other words, the final goal of sexuality functions as the end of desire, as the final quelling or silencing of the machines that keep on stirring up the entire question of desire again and again. Here we can see the body that is produced by phallic order is made of a particular metal. It is the metal body of the ego that is produced to enclose or encase the organs or partial objects; it is made to protect the ego from its own desiring-machine, in order to finally put a stop to them, as if to encase them in solid lead, thereby to cause them to stop working. In all this we must keep in mind that the desiring-machines do not belong to the body determined by the ego, but are distributed across several bodies, from the very beginning. This is why the ego's projection of the body, or of the phallic project of the body as the image of the ego (*Körper-Ich*) is essentially false and leads to constant suppression of the desiring-machines. In real sexuality, for example, to suppress the desiring-machine is nothing less than to suppress the part of the desiring-machine that exists in the other's body to which my desiring machine is connected and which it requires in order to function at all. This is why Deleuze posed the idea of jealousy that functions in Proust as crucial to determining the dialectic between the whole and the parts in sexuality, posed in terms of the subject of Marcel, and the partial objects that were scattered over and dwelled inside Albertine's body. Jealousy was the form of Marcel's recognition of the fugitive nature of partial objects that existed in the position of Albertine's body, and holding her captive was his manner of maintaining possession of them.

In all 'human sexual relationships', regardless of how you choose to arrange your organs into a desiring-machine, there is also a specific kind of talk of alienation as well that which directly addresses this machinic alterity. '*You have alienated me from my desiring-machine. You came into my universe with your sick phantasy and you reorganized my desiring-machine in order to get it to work according to your plan, and now my desiring-machine is all in pieces, broken and scattered about the floor like junk.*' But this accusation already follows the narrow path opened by blaming the parents. In other words, someone is always to blame – someone must take the blame, someone must be guilty! In some ways, this complaint is always true, which is why it is always difficult to dismiss it out of hand, leading the defendant to make constant rebuttals and demurs: Yes, it is true, you are alienated, you are not to be blamed for your loss of desire, but then I am not to be blamed either. I am really innocent in this whole affair. *We are both victims!* If the question becomes who is really to blame, or even if it is a question of blaming someone at all, it is this constant cycle of guilt and innocence as the two poles of Oedipal sexuality that is responsible for producing the end of desire. Why guilt, after all, if not to formulate the entire question of desire from the depressive position directly in relation to the law and its social tribunal? This is why sexual couples are always calling in the authorities to assist in the assigning of guilt, whether this amounts to actually calling the cops, or sending the accused to the doctor for evaluation, or in order to win their side of the argument, employing the language of psychoanalysis to diagnose the other's 'madness' or 'hysteria'.

In the end, of course, it does not really matter whether the cops come or not, since they are always just outside the window monitoring the situation, or they are in the neighbours' apartment with their ears pressed up against the wall, making certain that things do not get out of hand, that everyone plays within the legal limits laid down by the law. *All the while the couples themselves sit at the kitchen table, in their black robes, passing little death sentences on one another.* It is all quite 'Kafkaesque'!

Throughout *Anti-Oedipus* there is a constant refrain of blame and accusation as well, which can be formulated according to the statement that appears in Guattari's journals: 'An oedipal adult comes and sticks his gaze – even his hands and whatever else – into the Universe (in a set theory sense) of a child's a-conscious desiring machines' (AOP: 292). When Guattari refers to the adult 'in a set theory sense', he is referring to the entire adult–child series that traverses every social relation; thus, if the phallus instigates the original dualistic break between the sexes in terms of the primary social division, then it determines the original inequality as a kind of 'leftover energy' that is directly invested in every other social relation. Recalling the insight from Marx, inequality actually represents an original violence that effected this break, which is then converted into the form of legal violence, providing the energy to the social and technical machines that reproduce this division at every level of society. In this case, even behind the *imago* of the parent, there is already the instance of an original inequality in the presence of an adult who precedes and subordinates the parent to another series in the position of the child. This is why even the paranoid father who Oedipalises the child is actually found to be innocent of instigating this original violence and, in actuality, becomes a pathetic or passive subject; hence, the importance of Kafka's *Letter to His Father* for Deleuze and Guattari, where the father is actually found to be innocent. In fact, at the end of the long trial, both father and son are acquitted and appear equally as victims, even as accomplices; unfortunately, it is the mother who is finally to blame, or women in general (for example, the fiancée) and again the cycle of guilt and blame is not resolved, but merely displaced onto a third party. Technically, or legally, abstract equality can only be produced by displacing an original inequality onto a third. Thus, behind every social couple there is another, more primitive couple, but this more primitive couple is defined by an original inequality. Behind the sexual couple, there are the parents, but behind the parents, there is the couple defined by the inequality of the classes. Even earlier in the work on Sacher-Masoch, Deleuze will already discover masochistic couples functioning more like doubles or co-conspirators against a third term which represents the law.

Today, on the other hand, the sexual relation is fundamentally governed by what Freud referred to earlier on as 'a masochistic trend in instinctual life'. This can also be confirmed by Deleuze's constant reference to the status of the law and the contract in terms of the modern world that is fragmented and not ruled by *logos*. Consequently, the problem of the law appears as a formidable unity or as a primary power that controls the world of untotalisable fragments. 'The law no longer says what is good, but good is what the law says' ('it is good because I say it is'), revealing an order that is absolutely empty, uniquely formal, because it causes us to know no distinct object, no Good of reference, no 'referring Logos' (P: 131). This uniquely formal and empty form would be equivalent to the determination of the 'good' in a masochistic order; thus, 'I say it is good, meaning pleasurable, because I say it is', even though the position of the 'I' does not refer to any particular subject, as it does in sadism, and certainly not to the one who possesses the phallus (as in a phallocentric order), but rather functions like a 'shifter' in speech act theory that only refers to the one who is speaking, who is saying that it is because that is how it works, that is how the good is produced for me. What I mean by this is that the sexual relation, regardless of gender or sexuality, is very much understood today as a kind of contract, even a sexual constitution that has a peculiar relationship to the discourse of rights. It is for this reason that the question of classifying certain kinds of sexuality as perversions is almost nonsensical, because sexuality is no longer governed by a dominant form of right, and as long as there exists the presence of something like a constitution at the basis of any arrangement of sexuality, it is legally sanctioned and more or less democratic. We all fuck like lawyers these days. This is why I had described that the entire question of fucking today is one of jurisprudence in four different areas: formally, practically, legally and ethically. Formally, the sexual relationship must be conducted in such a manner that it is recognised as sexuality by both or all parties; practically, it must be possible for each party to achieve *jouissance*; legally, it must be something to which all parties must give their consent; finally, naturally it must reflect the ethical principles of the society to which it belongs, whether or not it be determined good or bad under these same principles. In fact, the current masochistic arrangement has almost the same formal structure as the Kantian formula of moral duty: that everything is allowed as long as I consider the other's body as an end in itself (the presence of humanity in the person) and should not be treated as a means to satisfying my own end. Of course, this would be what Kant defined as a hypothetical imperative and not as a categorical imperative, since there are constant exceptions and compromise formations where a purely temporary form of subordination is accepted in exchange for another, breaches of treaty, negotiations, petitions which have replaced commands of an absolutist order, which is that of the sadist.

Ontologically, the problem of the couple precedes the sexual couple as such; this is something that Deleuze clearly shows in *Logic of Sense*. Moreover, if every sexual couple hides a more primitive social pair, it goes without saying that this primary couple is not the parents. In a nutshell, this is the major thrust of the argument of *Anti-Oedipus*, since it is Oedipus that blocks discovery of new couples by placing the parents at the beginning of the social division. (Here, Deleuze and Guattari echo Lacan in following the French verbal permutations of *separer*, *se separare*, in the sense of to cause oneself to be engendered.) Consequently, it may very well be that perversion exists, structurally, by means of separating desire from its object-cause, and this entails a disavowal of the sexes (i.e., perversion has been defined as the disavowal of castration as an event that determines the object-cause of desire). In masochism, castration does not pre-exist and does not form the beginning of the sexual series, which is why it must constantly be produced as something effectively existing and, moreover, something that is real for the subject. Nevertheless, this is in order to seek a more primary couple that is already operating beneath the symbolic organisation of sexual desire.

Sexuality – in *all* cases – only constitutes a 'partial solution' to the dialectic of the primary social couple, by projecting its unconscious phantasm over the surface of a body without organs that is composed of two different beings. Thus, in the conclusion of Michel Tournier's *Vendredi, ou les Limbes du Pacifique*, which Deleuze comments on in detail, the primary couple of Robinson and Friday are shown in the image of the Orphic egg that spins on its axis until the yoke is distributed across the surface of the body without organs. The problem of sexual differentiation will be one and the same – how to separate the yolk and the white, to cause the yoke to flow and distribute itself across a surface constituted by the phantasm, or to fold two surfaces together until they become 'united on a single side' (on a surface which is produced by the phantasm itself), in other words, to recall the famous joke by Lacan, how to make an 'hommelette'. In *Logic of Sense*, Deleuze writes:

> The phantasm returns to its beginning which remained external to it (castration); but to the extent that the beginning was itself the result, the phantasm also returns to that from which the beginning had resulted (the sexuality of the corporeal surfaces); and finally, little by little, it returns to the absolute origin from which everything proceeds (the depths). One could now say that everything – sexuality, orality, anality – receives a new form on the surface . . . Without this intrinsic repetition of beginnings, the phantasm could not integrate its other, extrinsic beginning. (LS: 219)

In the above passage, the disavowal of sexual difference is accompanied by the 'de-sexualisation' of the surface that had resulted from placing castration at the beginning, and this inevitably entails in some cases, or in some so-called perversions (if this term has any meaning for us today, which I have questioned), a redistribution of the sexuality of corporeal surfaces, a new polarisation of the former zones of pleasure and pain that had crisscrossed the body without organs. Such is the case of the famous 'coldness' that determines a masochist's body, which is better explained by 'the emergence of a new form that redistributes the previous zones of sexuality, orality, and anality' in such a way that the corporeal surface produced in masochism is more distant and remote, hard like metal, cool like leather, bright and shiny (in contrast to the attributes that defined the former surface which were proximate, soft and warm as the flesh, opaque and translucent). If this seems like a simple reversal of attributes, or a violent denegation of former attributes that determined the sexual object, this is because we must understand that the erogenous zones are always engaged in a violent combat, one which castration and the body constructed by the genital drives were supposed to pacify and become the permanent arbiter and despot (LS: 222–3).

As Deleuze reminds us, 'the genital zone is always the arena of a larger context on the level of the species and the entire humanity': the combat between the brain and the mouth. Sexuality appears as that crack that runs between the brain and the mouth, but it is more like a crack that appears in porcelain with a thousand tiny fingers that run in each direction, a vast and intricate network that may very well appear, on one side, 'like a language' since it is composed of a chain of semiotic flows connected to the material fluxes of partial objects. The thinker and the writer (and, in a certain sense, the masochist) are united in their goal of producing a more primary couple, and the problem for each is to construct a mode of the couple in thought without sinking back into the puerile associations and clichéd assertions 'about' sexuality, which only constructs a way of thinking the couple or even of becoming a couple via castration (separation, sexual division, lack, extrinsic relationship between desire and its object). Thus, throughout Deleuze's work there is always this tendency of the writer to begin or to affirm the position of the bachelor, or of the thinker to begin from a depressed position of solitude, just as the masochist must begin from a perverse position at least with regard to the Oedipal organisation of sexuality and 'human desire'. (Kafka only offers us the most unique example of all three positions: depressive, schizophrenic and the masochist.) But is this any different from those who begin or seek to begin again on the plane composed by their own sexuality, to become thinkers and artists, just as often as they also become victims of their own sad sexual militancy. Therefore, on the basis of the above dialectic, again we must recognise that the path via sexuality is never the final answer and more often than not leads to sadness and failure, since the sexual pair always obstructs the more primary couple, and sooner or later becomes an image or simulacrum that blocks any access to this couple, since it is only a superficial path on the way to the primary social division: between the human and non-human sex.

In conclusion, I come back to a crucial and well-known passage from *Anti-Oedipus* that defines the positive reality of the unconscious from three perspectives: the Cartesian body without organs, the Marxist materialist discovery of the true nature of production, and, lastly, materialist psychiatry and the an-Oedipal determination of the role of partial objects.

For the unconscious is an orphan, and produces itself within the identity of nature and man. The autoproduction of the unconscious suddenly became evident when the subject of the Cartesian cogito realized it had no parents, when the socialist thinker discovered the unity of man and nature within the process of production, and when the cycle discovers its independence from an indefinite parental regression. To quote Artaud again: '*I got no/papamummy*'. (AO: 49)

Here, we see the constant refrain given throughout *Anti-Oedipus*, which actually constitutes the metaphysical foundation of their entire philosophical project, a refrain that can equally be found in Deleuze's other writings such as *Difference and Repetition* and even in his early work on Proust: *It is only the category of multiplicity, without recourse to the predicative relation between One and the Many, that can account for real desiring production.* (Here, as an aside, we can see why Badiou misunderstood the metaphysical claim of Deleuze's entire system, since he failed to understand the true social nature of the problem: how to create multiplicity without recourse to the One and the Many. For example, Deleuze does not understand multiplicity as the singularly differentiated One that is infinitely differentiated in its parts, which function as its modes; multiplicity is not the predicative distribution of the One in all of its modes.) At the same time, the metaphysical pretention of a pure multiplicity is always related to a problem, if not the problem, which is immediately posed in terms of the current theorisation of the nature of desiring production: 'how to think, that is, to produce the various parts whose sole relationship to each other is sheer difference, that is, without recourse to an expression of the whole, neither as a nostalgic whole that has been lost, or a virtual whole that is still to come' (AO: 41).

In my view, the most crucial passage of *Anti-Oedipus* is the following where this problem is restated in the most material and even historical of terms:

> We live today in an age of partial objects, bricks that have been shattered to bits, and leftovers. We no longer believe in the myth of the existence of fragments that, like pieces of an antique statue, are merely waiting for the last one to turn up so that they may all be glued back together to create a unity that is precisely the same as the original unity. We no longer believe in a primordial totality that once existed, or in a final totality that awaits us at some future date. We no longer believe in the dull grey outlines of a dreary, colourless dialectic of evolution aimed at forming a harmonious whole out of heterogeneous bits by rounding off their edges. We believe in totalities that are peripheral. And if we discover such a totality alongside various separate part, it is a whole of these particular parts but does not totalize them; it is the unity of all these particular parts but does not unify them; rather it is added to them as a new part fabricated separately. (AO: 42)

On a materialist level, the problem of the One and the Many, or the whole and the parts, is not a purely metaphysical problem; on a social level it concerns the fragments that belong to any social organisation, how they fit together to form a whole, how they function and work together in a machine that determines the total productive capacity of a society. However, on a subjective and psychological level, the problem of the whole and the parts determines the entire meaning of sexuality;

although here, the parts are not individuals or sexes, but rather machines that must be fitted together according to some arrangement in order to work. The two levels, the social and productive and the subjective or psychological, are implicated in one another; the relationship is disjunctive, which means inclusive, even though the manner in which they communicate their contents is by a series of hermetically sealed boxes. In other words, it has the appearance that sexuality is sealed off from social production and its contents are private; however, this only provides the conditions for the positive discovery of the unconscious by psychoanalysis, that is, the manner in which contents communicate between the two levels.

Finally, let return now to the early text on Proust to find the same discussion of the relationship between the part and the whole, to the discourse on the three sexualities in Proust:

> The Proustian theory is extremely complex because it functions on several levels . . . The first level was defined by statistical entity of heterosexual loves. The second, by two homosexual (yet still statistical) series, according to which an individual considered within the preceding entity was referred to other individuals of the same sex . . . But the third level is transsexual ('which is very wrongly called homosexuality') and transcends the individual as well as the entity: it designates in the individual a co-existence of fragments of both sexes, partial objects that do not communicate. (P: 135–6)

Here we see that the precise shape of the desiring-machines, the bric-a-brac field of partial objects that function as desiring-machines, is precisely those fragments referred to above that must be pieced together or, more often than not, forced into place that they may or may not belong. Is this not, after all, a perfect description of sexuality, human and non-human alike, composed of different desiring-machines that may or may not belong together, but forced into any number of arrangements with larger technological and social machines, or, as in Kafka's case, bureaucratic and juridical machines. For example, today, through a certain constant violence, the child's body is always placed like a broken fragment into a relationship with the desiring-machines of the court, the school, the clinic. Moreover, today if someone's desiring-machine is not working, there is always the right prescription that will get the pieces into place and get them functioning according to a certain order that is equally prescribed: happiness, success, marriage, good diet, exercise and so on. Is this not a better manner of picturing the relationship of desire as well as the question of sexuality than the usual representations 'about' human sexuality? In other words, in posing the question of sexuality, 'human and all too human', one should simply ask: 'What are your desiring machines? How do they work? Even when they are not working?'

Notes

1. Althusser, *Écrits philosophiques et politiques: Tome I*, p. 450.
2. Ibid., p. 452.
3. Ibid., p. 453.

6. 'Becoming-Animal' and 'Territory'

To constitute a territory is for me very near to the origin of the work of art.
L'Abécédaire de Gilles Deleuze, 'A comme Animal'

In the first of the series of interviews with Claire Parnet, '*A comme Animal*', Deleuze makes some very telling statements concerning the relation between a territory and art that informs his notion of 'becoming-animal', which was first employed especially in reference to children and writers, and which is often described as a process similar to 'making a map of a territory' (A: 'A'). For Deleuze, while the animal has a privileged and very specific relation to the notion of territory, one that is based on a finite number of affects and on a process of selection (i.e., the extraction of singularities from a milieu or an environment [*Umwelt*]); by contrast, and in some way a reversal of Heidegger's formulation of poverty, the human is defined as a relation to world, but no relation to a distinctive territory (i.e., the human being has no proper territory of its own, and thus could be said to be poor in this particular relationship to an immediate environment). On the other hand, writers and artists are often described as beings who enter into a process of becoming where the subject loses its own proper identity as an individual member of the group or even species and thus enters into a process that closely approximates the animal's 'captivation' (*Benommenheit*), to employ Heidegger's term, even though the artist or the writer produces a specific territory by extracting lines, fragments, colours, visions or scenes from an external environment in order to compose a specific kind of territory that is 'captured' in the work of art, and which exhibits different variabilities depending on the medium employed. For example, by extracting lines, scenes, fragments, even words and images, the artist or writer 'deterritorialises' an external world, which is then reterritorialised onto the specific territory of the artwork. Returning to 'A is for Animal', Deleuze lists the three primary affects that can be located in the animal world – colour, line and song – but which can also be found in art, and this leads him directly to the statement given above in the epigraph that to constitute a territory is very close to the origin of the work of art (A: 'A').

However, we must first determine 'extraction' or 'selection' by a process that is different from what is called 'perception' in a psychological sense, which can only be applied in a metaphorical sense when referring to how cells perceive other cells, for example, or how plants and animals 'perceive' their environments via 'signals'. In fact, what Deleuze calls 'extraction of singularities' is not unlike the biological selection of a constellation of affective possibilities that determine the animal's relation to the environment purely in terms of active and passive affects that compose the animal's body as already an intrinsically structured relation to an environment. In the plateau 'Becoming-intense, becoming-animal', Deleuze and Guattari employ the comparative psychology of ethology, especially Uexküll's semiotic theory, the Stoic theory of signs, and, finally, Spinoza's ethical theory of parallelism; as a result of this strange mixture, a 'body' is not defined in terms of genus and species, but rather in terms of the total number of affects that define its capacity (which runs parallel with Spinoza's definition of *conatus*). As they write:

> In the same way that we avoided defining a body by its organs and functions, we will avoid defining it by Species or Genus characteristics; instead we will seek to count its affects. This kind of study is called ethology, and this is the sense in which Spinoza wrote a true Ethics. A racehorse is more different from a workhorse than a workhorse is from an ox. Von Uexküll, in defining animal worlds, looks for the active and passive affects of which the animal is capable in the individuated assemblage of which it is a part. (ATP: 257)

In other words, what Heidegger calls the 'eliminative character' of openness that is particular to animal captivation can be useful in defining a process that Deleuze calls 'extraction of a few singularities', which are usually small in number as is his choice of animals to illustrate this process – for example the tick, the flea or the louse. (Of course, it is this minimalism that will also transfer to his love of writers like Michaux and Beckett, who also expresses the tendency to construct a world from a few scraps.) However, my purpose for this comparison is nothing less than to demonstrate that what Deleuze and Guattari call 'becoming animal' may, in fact, be closely related to what Heidegger already identifies as the process of eliminative behaviour whereby he specific form of territory is first produced or is brought about (*errungen*) in the form of encirclement (*Umringen*), and in the following I will show that this is very close to what Deleuze calls the process of the extraction of singular attributes by which both children and artists also make a territory,

Usually when one speaks of territories, there is already an implicit reference to cartography and the art of making maps. But what are maps made for? In response, they are made to fashion the relation between territory and a world. In other words, maps already provide us with a vivid demonstration of the process of 'deterritorialization–reterritorialization'. Here, one might think of a series of colourful maps that show the territorial constellations of Europe through the past two centuries, in which territories are drawn and redrawn as the results of wars, concessions, donations, treaties and alliances. In each series, there is an orientation towards a world that the map itself does not represent, but seems to provide the depth and volume that constitutes the force of an outside that causes the series to remain fragmentary and at the same time refer to something like a whole that is the object of the series, but yet is not a part of the map itself. It is from the creation of the perspective bird's-eye view that gazes over the map that all the territories are assembled to greet the eye, but nevertheless the eye itself does not naturally belong to the assemblage of the territories themselves but has been produced or projected above the geometrical surface of the map. Of course, it is also the perspective of geometric blocks projected over a smooth space, and in this regard we might suddenly see a resemblance to the point of view that is produced by the artwork described above, which cannot be reduced to any perspective that belongs to the environment from which it was drawn. It is what Deleuze calls, following the work of Kurt Lewin, 'haptic vision': 'the first aspect of the haptic, smooth space of close vision is that its orientations, landmarks, and linkages are in continuous variation; it operates step by step' (ATP: 493). However, it is also from this perspective that we might locate a difference with the animal's point of view in its own environment, to speak generically, or the differences between the drawings of children, and the territory of the artwork. The point of view produced by the work of art as a map is, in fact, a fourth affective possibility that is added to the first three that Deleuze defines as line, colour, song; it is the intensive affective possibility of movement that carries the first three affects along and produces an orientation away from and, at the same time, towards a world.

As I was writing this, I often visited the Leeum Museum of Art in

Seoul on several occasions to study the landscapes by painters of the Joseon period, because I have always been drawn to something in their distinctive style, which departs from Chinese landscapes around the same period. The mid- to late Joseon Dynasty coincides with the collapse of Ming Dynasty when China ceased to have pre-eminent cultural influence and Korean landscape painting took its own course and become increasingly distinctive in style and subject. Hence, a national painting style of landscape school called 'true view' began, moving from the traditional Chinese style of idealised general landscapes to particular and common locations rendered with an increased realism. As an example, I have provided a reference to a small landscape painting by a famous artist of the 'true view' movement, Gim Hong-do (1745–1806).[1]

In painting and watercolour, a landscape composes a specific kind of territory. And yet, as Deleuze argues, 'It is not enough to say that it is a landscape and that it lays out a place or territory.' But again, 'what it lays out are paths it is itself a voyage' (CC: 65). Thus, the perspective or point of view is always mobile and is made to orient the territory expressed by the work to a world that the artist or writer is either in the process of fleeing from or in the process of approaching or coming closer to be means of an intensive rather than an extensive movement, which can be illustrated simply be the affective movement of vision or sensation that some works produce to cause a simple perception to suddenly appear from a more intensive point of view that approximates a vision, or simply in the manner that certain psychological emotions can become intensified by a musical territory or composition, suddenly releasing new affective possibilities into the environment. Recalling the earlier discussion of the process of 'extraction of singularities' from *L'Abécédaire*, these singularities are extracted from an environment (a world) and then composed in the form of a territory that refers to both extensive and intensive states (i.e., both in the world and from the imagination, but at the point of their mutual becoming and transformation, or what Deleuze will call their 'crystallisation'). Therefore, if the voyage refers to the process of extraction, then territories in painting would also be composed in this manner and we would need to find something that resembles the singular 'thisness' that defines a landscape in order to discover something comparable to a voyage or a walk.

Gim Hong-do also painted crowded scenes of common people or, as in the case of the landscape with wild geese, his paintings have a postcard or photographic realism in a palette of whites, blues and greens.

Yet, yet if every landscape is not simply a laying-out of a simple territory or place that exists already beforehand, but is only composed through a process of extraction of singularities, producing a mobile perspective, or vision, then what could be the equivalent of Gim Hong-do's composition? Here, the process of extraction is clearly visible in the sense that only a few elements are extracted from an environment or world in order to compose the territory (rocks, a river, geese, shadows, the trace of wind or breeze on the water). In the painted landscape a territory bleeds through the paper, but does not represent a world that exists beforehand; rather, it expresses a singular point of view.

Next, we need to consider the poem that appears next to the scene in the upper left-hand corner of the painting. It is a traditional Chinese poem that also expresses an haecceity, a singular moment of apprehending nature, in an expression that is both extensive and intensive at once. Consequently, all the elements relate to one another in a singular composition that expresses an intensive state, pure feeling: the water running down from the mountain, the descending mist, the breeze that creases or makes ripples in the water. There is the feeling of a shudder that might come over the viewer, a shudder that is like that of wild geese flapping their wings, a feeling of intensity that circulates and connects the body to the landscape. One might also imagine this scene of the wild geese on the water is as much a depiction of the body of Gim Hong-do as the particular landscape. In other words, it is perhaps in this way that we might determine the equivalent of a 'voyage' in landscape painting, referring to the merging of an intensive state with the external environment, but in a manner that creates or produces a distinctive territory that could not exist either outside the painting or before. For example, neither the landscape nor the poem are intended to represent the feeling of the shudder described above, but only the relation that is produced BETWEEN the affective body and the environment (or the world).

Does the body I am defining refer to the body of the painter, the actual body of Gim, Hong-do? No, because it is now a body composed in its own territory, which now also includes the rocks, the river, the wild geese, the wind, as well as the lines of the poem. It is what Deleuze calls elsewhere an an-organic body, but one that is no less real than the organically composed body, except that it is purely intensive, which is to say, a specific constellation of singular affects. In this regard, it is a body that is no different from the 'becoming-horse' of Little Hans (a body that is composed of the intensives affects that Little Hans extracts from his voyage into the street). In other words, the painter and the writer, in this case, just like the animal and the child, explore their milieu by what Deleuze calls 'dynamic trajectories' and by making maps of these dynamic trajectories. A territory is a map of specific kind, and what I am referring to as a 'body' exists only as a territory that is expressed by the work of art, using its own medium and possibilities, but the process in both media closely approximates what Deleuze earlier referred to as the 'extraction of singularities', producing a crystalline perception that can in no way resemble natural perception.

When it comes to the question of the specific territory produced by the artwork, we cannot employ the maps that are drawn to represent any kind of territory. Again, there must be a specific kind of map that the artwork emulates or composes in orienting itself towards the world. For example, let us think only of a territory in language, in writing, and of a very particular map, the psychic maps that are often drawn by children. It is especially in Deleuze and Guattari's use of the maps created by children, such as Fannie Deleuze, or especially the psychic maps like those of the Wolf Man or Little Hans – or, as I will return to in the conclusion, of Leonardo da Vinci – that we will also see an immediate comparison with the territory of the animal, if only because the maps of children are often filled with animals, like the Wolf Man's vision of a tree full of wolves was in fact a drawing of a psychic landscape. In fact, they constitute a living ecological picture that is often more accurate than ethological or comparative biology in picturing what kind of life inhabits a given environment. So we now see that the maps that Deleuze is referring to here resemble those by children or in painting rather than geographical maps, but one can just as easily speak of the specific territorial maps made up by writing and literature, as in the case of so-called 'national literatures' as when we say 'American Literature' or 'German Literature' (although, I would argue, these territories may also resemble more the maps drawn by children than geographical maps). Moreover, we could easily substitute the term 'writers' for 'children' in the statement that writers never stop exploring milieus by means of dynamic trajectories and drawing up maps of them. 'In its own way', therefore, 'all art says what children say. It is made up of trajectories and becomings, and it too makes maps, both extensive and intensive. There is always a trajectory in the work of art' (CC: 65–6). However, something is added to the map produced by children and writers (or works of art in general) that Deleuze defines as a 'dynamic trajectory', which, in turn, will relate a milieu (an environment, a territory) to psychic activity. However, 'Maps should not be understood only in extension, in relation to a space constituted by trajectories. There are also maps of intensity, of density, that are concerned with what fills temporal and psychic spaces, what subtends the trajectory'; moreover, 'just as trajectories are no more real than becomings are imaginary, there is something unique in their joining together that belongs only to art' (CC: 64).

But what is a trajectory, which appears as the essential perspective (i.e., 'there are always trajectories . . .') that is introduced by the artwork? In the original French, the terms *trajet* and *trajectoire* (pathway and trajectory, or direction) are always placed alongside the term *parcours* (route, journey, distance covered). Deleuze also gives the terms an intensive as well as an extensive usage; therefore, the route, the journey and the distance covered do not only refer to the extensive sense that is measurable in terms of space and time, but also to an intensive and dynamic sense of 'becoming', that is, as a psychic journey in which the route and the distance covered refer to an intensive process of affection. It is in this sense that Deleuze defines the sense of the phrase 'becoming-animal' in reference to the case study of Little Hans in a manner that will allow us to define the 'becoming-horse' of the child as a 'dynamic trajectory' of a specific kind. Examining the trajectory of Little Hans, what is the map he makes of his environment, which Deleuze opposes to the parental or Oedipal map of Little Hans's 'intensive journey'? Deleuze often utilises the same definition of the 'body' that he employed with regard to the world expressed by Uexküll and Spinoza, that is, a body that is not defined according to genus or species (in other words, there is no 'horse' strictly speaking), but rather in terms of active and passive affects:

> Little Hans defines a horse by making out a list of its affects, both active and passive: having a big widdler, hauling heavy loads, having blinkers, biting, falling down, being whipped, making a row with its feet. It is this distribution of affects (with the widdler playing the role of a transformer or convener) that constitutes a map of intensity. It is always an affective constellation. (CC: 65)

What is the function of 'a horse' in Hans's psychic journey other than what Deleuze elsewhere calls a body without organs? That is to say, it is 'a body' that is partly created by Hans's psychic activity in which the horse is reassembled like a mechanism or a machine and redefined in terms of active and passive affects that are immediately linked to the

environment that Hans discovers, an environment that is now immediately connected to what is happening in his body, to his 'becoming-
animal'. Consequently, even the organs are reorganised and reclassified
and no longer correspond to the genus and species determination of the
animal in a biological classification. Instead, there is a list or a 'table' of
affects, and of new signs, that compose this marvellous creature, and
in many ways, the relation of these new affects function in the same
way as the three affects that define a tick's relation to its environment.
Therefore, it is in this manner that the 'becoming-animal of Little Hans'
can be defined, and it is also in the same manner that an artist extracts
singularity from his or own environment to create a new territory.

Perhaps now we might understand the relation between 'trajectory' (in an extensive sense) and 'becoming' (as an intensive voyage or
journey). In the example of Little Hans, it is the intensive movement
that is effected by 'becoming-horse' that Little Hans bears a trajectory
that departs from the family house as he begins to map a new territory
represented by the streets and all the affective possibilities that can be
connected to this new territory that is linked to his 'impulse of intensity',
whether this is registered in terms of new fears or new affective possibilities of desire. It is for this reason that the parents are opposed to Little
Hans's 'psychic journey' towards the street and away from the parental
world. As Deleuze writes:

> Hans's becoming-horse refers to a trajectory, from the apartment house
> to the warehouse. The passage alongside the warehouse, or even the visit
> to the henhouse, may be customary trajectories, but they are not innocent
> promenades. We see clearly why the real and the imaginary were led to
> exceed themselves or even to interchange with each other: a becoming is not
> imaginary, any more than a voyage is real. It is becoming that turns the most
> negligible of trajectories, or even a fixed immobility, into a voyage; and it is
> the trajectory that turns the imaginary into a becoming. There are two types
> of maps, those of trajectories and those of affects, refers to the other. (CC: 65)

Of course, as Deleuze also says, in part agreeing with Freud's earlier
theory of the libido, the 'widdler' represents the introduction of dynamic
perspective in the psychic landscape of 'Little' Hans, will provide all
the energy for the psychic journey that takes place, and there is a hint
at what Little Hans is seeking through a creation of a new trajectory
that immediately relates his newly discovered 'body' to a territory that
exists outside the parents' home – a territory, moreover, that has been

prohibited by the parents and directly opposes the parental desire to keep him shut up in the apartment, but also to prevent his eyes from seeing what is going on out there in the streets, the warehouses, in the henhouse. After all, what might Little Hans actually witness in these new territories but all kinds of sordid affairs not only between animals but also among the other classes with whom Little Hans has been forbidden to come into contact and who are often compared to animals at the dinner table (at least, one might imagine)? Hans would immediately perceive the truth of desire, or the truth of sexuality (both human and animal), but this is not what is important, because Hans knows nothing of this reality, but only that there is a another territory that intensely interests him and he seeks to map it and connect it directly to the intensive movement of desire that courses throughout his body and immediately – one might say – immanently connects him to this new territory.

As Deleuze says, '[T]he map expresses the identity of the journey and what one journeys through. It merges with its object, when the object itself is movement' (CC: 61). Thus, this is the trajectory and the territory that merge together in Little Hans's desire, in his real intensive journey of 'becoming-horse'. In other words, the map of the territory made up by the trajectory of Little Hans expresses the identity of the subjectivity with the movement of becoming. But why does Deleuze constantly also say that trajectories are not real, but only to the same degree that becomings are not imaginary? In fact, this defines the intensive sense of the trajectory, since Hans did not make an extensive journey into the territory, but rather he created a territory that was not imaginary because it contains other beings that are real (horses, animals, other classes, noises of the streets, other enclosures that were as differentiated from the family home as a warehouse or a henhouse). It is here we might find the connection to the intensive journeys and to the territories created by writers and artists. Simply put, do writers not also make intensive journeys that are not real but which, at the same time, are not imaginary either? In other words, does not art also produce a trajectory 'that turns the imaginary into a becoming'?

Now that we have defined the dynamic trajectory of the intensive journey that determines the sense of 'becoming-animal' in the case of Little Hans, we must return to one nagging question: the question concerning the 'widdler'. In the end, even Deleuze could not get around its centrality in providing the unconscious energy of investment that transforms perception and the imaginary into a new affective territory.

Consequently, there is a 'vision' (which psychoanalysis demotes to the role of phantasy and defines strictly according to the term of the imaginary) functions both as a virtual object and a real affect inscribed on the body with organs, as Deleuze and Guattari will call this intensive plane in *Anti-Oedipus*. Thus,

> At the limit, the imaginary is a virtual image that is interfused with the real object, and vice versa, thereby constituting a crystal of the unconscious. It is not enough for the real object or the real landscape to evoke similar or related images; it must disengage its own virtual image at the same time that the latter, as an imaginary landscape, makes its entry into the real, following a circuit where each of the two terms pursues the other, is interchanged with the other. 'Vision' is the product of this doubling or splitting in two [*doublement ou dedoublement*], this coalescence. It is in such crystals of the unconscious that the trajectories of the libido are made visible. (CC: 63)

Nevertheless, we must come back to the same question I asked before: does the choice of objects that the unconscious libido invests in always have to do with the sexualised body, or be determined sexually? Accordingly, this would simply condemn the territories created by artists and writers to simply be metaphors of the parental bodies, and the function of art itself and its intensification of affect to a question of the sublimation of sexual energy.

As in Freud's interpretation of Leonardo da Vinci, sublimation involves the devaluation of an immediate sexual aim, which in some special cases assumes the form of a sexualisation of the organs of perception and thought with 'the special intensity of an impulse', which in Leonardo's case, is an impulsive curiosity about the natural world. In particular, this curiosity takes as its privileged objects the bodies of people and animals, which are constantly drawn and examined, both in terms of their external proportions and differences, but also in the extensive diagrams of their internal parts, their organs, including a detailed investigation of their biological functions. It is in this sense, according to Freud's theory, the impulse for curiosity finds its origin in the infantile scene of sexuality, and specifically in a traumatic event that threatens the infantile ego, which Freud later recounts in his interpretation of the vulture phantasy. In one stroke, Freud's theory explains both the nature and the cause of the infinite reservoir of sexual energy needed to sustain Leonardo's investigations into the natural world and the internal nature of bodies and objects, and, at the same time, he gives an explanation of the unfinished state of many of his artworks (and paintings, in particular) as being a repetition of the failure of his first infantile investigation concerning the riddle of man, *inter faeces et urinam nascimur*. Thus, Leonardo's habit of leaving things in a state of incompletion, also frequently noted by his biographers, now finds its cause in the impression of his failure to gain perfect intellectual independence from the accidental nature of his own sexuality, or to sublimate the intensity of its impulse into knowledge in the manner of Spinoza, who perhaps represents the most complete and perfect example of sublimated mind. Of course, in the case of da Vinci it is the particular fate of this unconscious affect to undergo repression, but as a result of which it is also fated to return to constitute the 'dynamic trajectory' that appears in most of Leonardo's portraits, but especially those of his later years, in which, Freud argues, the return of Leonardo's sexual intensity is more pronounced and assumes a form where this intensive affect is incorporated into the paintings as an anamorphic stain rather than becoming the cause of their incompletion. For example, this stain appears as the grotesque and slightly twisted smile of Mona Lisa that bears an entire series of phallic transfigurations of the body – that is, the lips of the infantile mouth sucking the nipple of a nursemaid, the mouth of the mother repeatedly kissing young Leonardo affectionately, becomes the male penis inserted into the mouth of the young Leonardo, the image of Leonardo's penis in the mouth of one of his young models, and, finally, the image provided by the phantasy of the tail (*coda*) of a vulture lashing against an open mouth.

In the above example of Leonardo's investigation into the mysteries of the human body, we have provided another example of what Deleuze identifies as a 'voyage' that constitutes the inorganic and yet living territory of the artwork. Therefore, we also find that the investigation in Leonardo's case, just as we found in Little Hans, would necessarily be motivated by an intensive and passionate curiosity about the external world, but might we also locate a threat also in the original impulse to flee from something else? In the case of da Vinci, there is a flight from female sexuality itself, which motivated the voyage to begin with, which later manifests itself as a superabundant and creative force coupled with an intensive 'line of flight' from a determined sexuality to an indeterminate and sublimated form of thought and becoming. This represents perhaps a fourth path of the libido in fashioning two conflicting images of rationality: on the one hand, obsessive compulsive thinking (the sexualization of the act of thinking itself) and, on the other, a complete desexualisation of the object of thought, as in purely formal rationality.

If we have already noted the tendency of certain animals to instinctively map their relation to their environments in terms of a territory made up of active and passive affects, this may also signal the first moment of the 'becoming-animal' of the child, as also in the example of a Little Hans. The distinction between human and animal from a psychoanalytic perspective may come down to the peculiar morphology of the sexual instinct in the human animal: what appears instinctual in most animals (that is, the determination of the sexual instinct) in humans originates from the vicissitudes of a quite arbitrary and accidental encounter with its own sexuation as a species-being, that is, its own morphogenesis. From Freud's observation, we are reminded that this encounter is so indeterminate that it may or may not occur for every individual of the species – in fact, it may not occur at all in some singular instances – and in those cases where it does occur, the effects on morphology of the individual will be quite variable and ultimately dependent precisely upon the first encounter with sexuality itself, which always comes before the child is ready for the experience, a fact that will later prepare the event for repression, as well as the birth of a certain moral faculty that is predominant in the human animal that will later blame one of the parents for its own state of initial 'prematurity' (i.e., 'sexism', since, historically, it is first the mother, and the woman in general, who is assigned this guilt by both sexes). At the same time, in a more positive spirit of Enlightenment, following Freud's account of the figures of da Vinci and Spinoza, it is from this accidental encounter that we also bear witness to the birth of the metaphysical instinct in the human animal, or, at least, to the beginnings of 'scientific investigation' into the 'mysteries of life' as well as 'the origin of the species'.

But let us take a less psychoanalytic path around the same problem of sublimation at the origin of the artistic process of producing or creating an artistic territory. We have been arguing all along that the sudden intensification of the body that we have found in the example of Little Hans corresponds to the sense of what Deleuze defines as a 'voyage' that results in the process of mapping (or remapping) the body's relation to its own environment in the manner of the animal, a process in which territory defined by active and passive affects are then mapped back onto an external environment (a street, a landscape). However, it is not arbitrary that we have also discovered that a particular animal has been involved in each case as well, which might even constitute a hypothetical principle of 'becoming-animal', that is, for understanding a new affective body that is produced through this process of deterritorialisation: 'a horse' for Little Hans; 'wolves' for the Wolf Man; finally, 'a kite' for Leonardo da Vinci. But what are these animals doing here, and what is their exact semiotic status? In fact, are they actually animals at all, or, as in Freud's interpretation, merely symbolic and partly mythological creatures that are constructed by the unconscious phantasy to represent the repressed infantile sexuality for each case? Or do they represent something else? In fact, are they made to represent anything at all, and if not, then what is their function? Here, we are reminded of Deleuze and Guattari's constant complaint against Freud for being too symbolic and always reducing the appearance of real animals to serving as representatives of the parents. 'A horse!' says Little Hans. 'Daddy!' says Freud. 'Wolves!' says the Wolf Man. 'Both Mummy and Daddy, *coitus a tergo*!' says Freud. 'A kite!' writes Leonardo in his journal. 'Vulture,' says Freud, who ultimately represents 'Mummy' (*Mutter*)! It is not only feminists and queer theorists who are still so angry at Freud for being both so literal and symbolically minded (as well as misogynistic, homophobic, heteronormative, etc.), but now it appears that animals are offended by psychoanalysis too. However, contrary to the moral indignation of Freud's critics, we also need to recall that precisely in these moments Deleuze and Guattari always begin to laugh, but also to report that it is not only they who are laughing, but children and animals are laughing as well. 'When psychoanalysis talks about animals, animals learn to laugh' (ATP: 240). It is even reported that, in the end, the Wolf Man realised that Freud did not know anything about zoology: 'He knew that Freud had a genius for brushing up against the truth and passing it by, then filling the void with associations. He knew that Freud knew nothing about wolves, or anuses for that matter. The only thing Freud understood was what a dog is, and a dog's tail' (ATP: 26).

Returning to the case of da Vinci, Freud interprets the phantasy of being wet-nursed by the mother (or her nurse) and finds that woman is later replaced by a vulture. But exactly where does this vulture first come into the picture? In order to resolve this mystery, Freud must pursue his investigation even further into the ancient past, leading him too scour through all the volumes reported to belong to Leonardo's library until he finds the *Codus Atlanticus* in the excerpts of Richter who details the volumes that Leonardo borrowed from his friends. Consequently, the exact volume that Freud was looking for turned out to be missing from da Vinci's own library, that is, an annotated and edited volume of Horapollo containing figures of the Egyptian deities, but especially the goddess Mut who is depicted with the head of a vulture, and in antiquity is described as bearing both sexual characteristics according to the common belief held at that time that all vultures were female and thus reproduced asexually. Therefore, 'in most representations the vulture-headed maternal deity was formed by the Egyptians in a phallic manner, her body which was distinguished as feminine by its breasts also bore the masculine member in a state of erection'.[2] *Voila!* At this point we might not only hear animals laughing – and vultures especially! – but the Egyptian gods as well. And if this was not enough, Freud cannot resist to offer one final association to the list: 'The name of this goddess was pronounced *Mut*; we may question whether the sound similarity to our word mother (*Mutter*) is only accidental?'[3] Of course, along with Freud, we can disregard the fact that the Egyptian word *mut* actually means 'mother' in Egyptian, which indeed sounds a lot like the German *Mutter*, since the etymological association between these two languages would probably not have had the same significance for the Renaissance Italian.

Nevertheless, one of the most remarkable aspects of his interpretation of the vulture phantasy in the essay on da Vinci is the great pains Freud takes to complicate the all too evident symbolic reading of the infantile reminiscence: tail of vulture = coda = breast = penis. This series is simply too obvious even for Freud, and we might even accept Freud's hypothesis that one of the sources of the vulture is drawn from his readings of the Church Fathers who often cite the passage from Horapollo concerning the fact that all vultures are female and reproduced without the assistance of the male member by spreading their wings, opening their vagina, and becoming impregnated by the wind.[4] The fact that this fable frequently appears in the writings of the Church Fathers concerning the immaculate conception of the Virgin Mother also makes it probable that it was an association that actually occurred to Leonardo as he was sketching various species of birds (including kites and hawks) in order to investigate the physics of flight. Thus, we can also accept Freud's interpretation of the nature of curiosity that appears both in the case of Little Hans and Leonardo, of the existence of an arbitrary encounter with sexuality that turns into the childhood exploration, at first, but then into an ongoing scientific investigation into 'where baby comes from.' Perhaps we must also modify the question to actually be directed towards the origin of the species as well, especially given that infantile theories concerning sexual reproduction also concern the question: 'What kind of animal am I?'

In Freud's own account, this origin is explained in terms of Leonardo's difficulty in accepting the humiliation of his own origins caused by his illegitimate birth and the absence of the father during the first five years of young Leonardo's life, which occasions the infantile theory of his immaculate conception by the wind and his later obsession with the subject of the Madonna and Child. All this fits neatly – too neatly, in fact! – and even though Freud's manner of finding an explanation for everything, and to put everything in its place in accordance with his own particular form of sublimation (which both sexualises thought and sublimates its sexual affect under a strict control of rationality). Nevertheless, despite both his tenacity and interpretive prowess, once again, Freud still remains both too literal and too symbolic in his interpretation of Leonardo's 'becoming-animal', which functions as something other than psychic compensation for his illegitimate birth (i.e., lack), for it gave him a special 'destiny' that is likened to the child of the Madonna as God's gift to humankind, which I will return to below, even though Leonardo's Madonna was the Egyptian female deity Isis (not *Mut*!), the wife-sister of Osiris who is frequently depicted in Egyptian hieroglyphs and statues as suckling her infant son Horus (the 'hawk-like' god of war).

Even though I have chosen to follow the path that was already laid out by Freud, we have ended up in purely speculative territory! It should not have escaped our notice, moreover, that there have been no animals at all in our discussion so far, only pieces and limbs, tails and beaks, of real animals. The vulture is not an animal in Freud's interpretation, but rather a mythological creature that belongs to infantile phantasy. In other words, it is only children and primitive religions that create animals like the figure of a human with the head of a vulture or a kite and a giant erection of a horse. We have all witnessed them in museums and across the dining-room table. And yet, it seems that children and ancient religions seem to know something about animals that Freud does not, which is their intensive zones and their external relations. These animals express something that is immediately mapped out onto the external world, as well as onto the entire past. Nevertheless, as Deleuze argues, 'The father and mother are not the coordinates of everything that is invested by the unconscious' (CC: 3). On the other hand, returning to Deleuze and Guattari's own treatment of animals, we must also now conclude that we do not find any real animals there either, at least not defined in terms of genus or species, but rather only 'animal-becomings', as we have already discovered above in the case of Little Hans. Instead, what we discover is that there are more demonic animals, pack or affect animals that form a multiplicity, a becoming, a population, a tale. Of course, there is always the possibility that a given animal, for example a louse, a cheetah or an elephant, will be treated as a pet. But Deleuze and Guattari may represent another pole, or an opposite extreme to psychoanalytic familialism: that it is also possible for any animal to be treated in the mode of the pack or swarm, that is to say, as 'fellow sorcerers' (ATP: 241). In fact, this might cause us to wonder if it is even possible for human beings – but especially adults! – to talk about real animals, that is, without reducing the animal to a human relation, including the relation of 'becoming'? After all, in Deleuze and Guattari's theory, it is only humans that become-animal, never the other way around. Animals do not become human, except in fairy tales and in Greek myths. And not even there! Even scientific knowledge presupposes an anthropomorphic motive of curiosity that we could very well apply to Freud's own insight that is not completely liberated from the first infantile investigations into the other life-forms that populate the immediate environment. In turn, we could also characterise much of the discussion that occurred recently in the field of the humanities (or the post-humanities) concerning the animal to show that behind or beneath these discussions and these knowledges is always the human relation, or the question of the human relation to the animal. In these discussions as well, nowhere does the animal appear to inhabit its own territory but is always found to be predisposed or to belong to the human world, even in a manner of being trapped or domesticated by the question of the human relation. Even wild and undomesticated animals are certainly not free of this world, as in the case of Deleuze and Guattari's privileged species, and always end up looking more or less like anti-Hegelians.

In concluding this brief meditation on the *human* question of territory actualised in the work of art, perhaps for this reason their entire theory of '*becoming x*' (-woman, -animal, -intensive, -imperceptible) is, after everything is said and done, a theory of sublimation, which is why Deleuze and Guattari so famously avoid sexuality, even find it repulsive as a theme (e.g., 'a dirty little secret'). Perhaps this is also why in 'A comme Animal', Deleuze confesses to Parnet such disdain, even disgust, for 'animals that rub up against him', for Oedipalised animals and family pets, which always represent a certain overflowing of libidinal energy that is prohibited to be exchanged between members of the family. For example, the love and cuddling of pets represents a manner of transferring erotic energy between family members through the intermediary of a transitional object, the family pet. This, in the final analysis, is why they particularly hate psychoanalysis, and the Freudian school especially: because it reduces everything to sexuality itself, *Ding an sich*, whereas they want to create a line of escape to turn the world into an intensive line of flight that directly leads outside, as in the case of Little Hans. However, what is the famous avoidance or defence of castration in perversion if not multiplication? In order to defend against its lethal meaning for the subject, the identification of the phallus is multiplied, and its effect is diverted away from the symbolic form and invested in the one of the other senses. Multiplication must not be understood numerically, but as a pixilation of the perceptual field, as in video, or as in the case of an expressionist technique of rendering an object through a thousand tiny brushstrokes.

The phallus may very well *not be the penis*, but according to Freud's own observation early on, this might be owed to the fact that one of the most primitive defences against the threat of castration is the multiplication of the feared object into a thousand tiny splinters, or, in Deleuze and Guattari's phrase, 'a thousand tiny sexes'. Nevertheless, it is also true that each of these splinters will retain their sexual energy both in thought and intensity, whether this energy assumes a form of obsessional thinking – that is, the sexualisation of thinking itself as forever 'incomplete and fragmentary' – which, in psychoanalytic theory, also belongs to obsessional neurosis, as intensive, and to perversion, as multiplicity of phallic substitutes – thus, *a thousand tiny widdlers*! For example, in employing da Vinci's own intensive map as a guide, we might ask whether or not a scientific investigation is simply a 'voyage' of a different kind, and in what manner scientific investigations produce or create maps that are different from artistic images of nature or territory. The fact that both the development of science and art still repeat the question over the 'accident at the origin of creation' is a fact that both unites them as two branches of a tree that grew from the same traumatic event, and condemns them to a certain failure, whether this is registered affectively as 'theoretical wonder' (*theoria*) or 'creative obsession'. In other words, both science and art originate from the same traumatic event of sexual difference. As Freud concludes in his psychoanalytic investigation of da Vinci:

> We are naturally grieved over the fact that a just God and a kindly providence do not guard us better against such influences in our most defenseless age. We thereby gladly forget that as a matter of fact everything in our life is accident from our very origin through the meeting of spermatozoa and ovum, accident, which nevertheless participates in the lawfulness and fatalities of nature and lacks only the connection to our wishes and illusions. The division of life's determinants into the 'fatalities' of our constitution and the 'accidents' of our childhood may still be indefinite in individual cases, but taken altogether one can no longer entertain any doubt about the importance of precisely our first years of childhood. We all still show too little respect for nature, which in Leonardo's deep words recalling Hamlet's speech 'is full of infinite reasons which never appeared in experience.' Every one of us human beings corresponds to one of the infinite experiments in which these 'reasons of nature' force themselves into experience.[5]

Notes

1. Gim Hong Do, *Wild Geese*, https://images.app.goo.gl/cTmP4dryN3M-Pr9yU8 (last accessed 12 August 2020).
2. Freud, Leonardo da Vinci and a Memory of His Childhood, p. 47.
3. Ibid., p. 48.
4. *Horapollinis Niloi Hieroglyphica edidit Conradus Leemans Amstelodami*, 1835. The words referring to the sex of the vulture read as follows (p. 14): 'μητέρα μὲν ἐπειδὴ ἄρρεν ἐν τούτω γένει τώων οὐχ ὑπάρχει.'
5. Freud, *Leonardo da Vinci and a Memory of His Childhood*, p. 100.

Bibliography

Adorno, Theodore, *Aesthetic Theory*, trans. Robert Hullot-Kentor, Minneapolis: University of Minnesota Press, 1997.

Agamben, Giorgio, *The Open: Man and Animal*, trans. Kevin Attell, Palo Alto: Stanford University Press, 2004.

Althusser, Louis, *Pour Marx*, Paris: Maspero, 1965.

Althusser, Louis, *Écrits philosophiques et politiques: Tome I*, Paris: Stock/IMEC, 1994.

Aristotle, *The Complete Works of Aristotle*, vol. 2, ed. Jonathan Barnes, Princeton: Princeton University Press, 1984.

Banfield, Ann, *The Phantom Table: Woolf, Fry, Russell and the Epistemology of Modernism*, Cambridge: Cambridge University Press, 2007.

Bergson, Henri, *The Creative Mind: An Introduction to Metaphysics* [1934], trans. Mabelle L. Andison, Mineola, NY: Dover Publications, 2007.

Bergson, Henri, *An Introduction to Metaphysics*, trans. T. E. Hulme, New York and London: G. P. Putnam's sons, 1910.

Derrida, Jacques (1976), *Of Grammatology*, trans. Gayatri Chakravorty Spivak, New York: Columbia University Press.

Derrida, Jacques, *The Other Heading: Reflections on Today's Europe*, Bloomington: Indiana University Press, 1992.

Derrida, Jacques, 'Faith and Knowledge: The Two Sources of "Religion" at the Limits of Reason Alone', *Religion*, ed. Gianni Vattimo, Stanford: Stanford University Press, 1998.

Derrida, Jacques, *The Beast and the Sovereign, Vol. 2*, trans. Geoffrey Bennington, Chicago: Chicago University Press, 2009.

Escudero, Jesús Adrián, 'Heidegger's *Black Notebooks* and the Question of Anti-Semitism', *Gatherings: The Heidegger Circle Annual* 5 (2015), 21–49.

Evans, Gareth, 'The Causal Theory of Names', *The Philosophy of Language*, ed. A. Martinich, Oxford: Oxford University Press, 1985, pp. 635–56.

Foucault, Michel, *Ethics: Subjectivity and Truth*, trans. R Hurley, New York: The New Press, 1997.

Freud, Sigmund, *Leonardo da Vinci and a Memory of His Childhood*, The Standard Edition: Complete Psychological Works of Sigmund Freud, W.W. Norton, 1990.

Gillies, Mary Ann, *Bergson and British Modernism*, Montreal: McGill Queen's University Press, 1996.

Gutting, Gary, 'Bridging the Continental Divide', *New York Times*, 12 Feb. 2012.

Guyer, P., 'Introduction: The Starry Heavens and the Moral Law', in *The Cambridge Companion to Kant and Modern Philosophy*, ed. P. Guyer, Cambridge Companions to Philosophy, Cambridge: Cambridge University Press, 2006, pp. 1–27.

Hardt, Michael, *Gilles Deleuze: An Apprenticeship in Philosophy*, Minneapolis: University of Minnesota Press, 1993.

Hardt, Michael and Antonio Negri, *Empire*, Cambridge, MA: Harvard University Press, 2000.

Heidegger, Martin and Bernd Magnus, 'Who is Nietzsche's Zarathustra?' *The Review of Metaphysics* 20:3 (1967), 411–31.

Heidegger, Martin, *What is Called Thinking?*, New York: Harper & Row, 1968.

Heidegger, Martin, *The Fundamental Concepts of Metaphysics: World, Finitude, Solitude*, trans. William McNeill and Nicholas Walker, Bloomington: Indiana University Press, 1995.

Kant, Immanuel, *Critique of the Power of Judgment*, trans. Paul Guyer and Eric Matthews, Cambridge: Cambridge University Press, 2000.

Kant, Immanuel, *Perpetual Peace and Other Essays*, trans. Ted Humphrey, Indianapolis: Hackett, 1983.

Kant, Immanuel, *Universal Natural History and Theory of the Heavens*, trans. Stanley L. Jaki, Edinburgh: Scottish Academic Press, 1981.

Kirk, G. S., and J. E. Raven, *The Pre-Socratic Philosophers*, Cambridge: Cambridge University Press, 1957.

Kripke, Saul, *Naming and Necessity*, Cambridge, MA: Harvard University Press, 1980.

Lacan, Jacques, *Four Fundamental Concepts of Psychoanalysis*, ed. Alan Sheridan, London: Penguin Books, 1977.

Lambert, Gregg, *In Search for a New Image of Thought: Gilles Deleuze and the Philosophy of Expressionism*, Minneapolis: University of Minnesota Press, 2012.

Lambert, Gregg, *The Non-Philosophy of Gilles Deleuze*, London: Continuum, 2002.

Lambert, Gregg, *Philosophy After Friendship: Deleuze's Conceptual Personae*, Minneapolis: University of Minnesota Press, 2017.

Lambert, Gregg, *Return Statements: The Return of Religion in Contemporary Philosophy*, Edinburgh: Edinburgh University Press, 2017.

Lucian, *The Downward Journey or The Tyrant. Zeus Catechized. Zeus Rants. The Dream or The Cock. Prometheus. Icaromenippus or The Sky-man. Timon or The Misanthrope. Charon or The Inspectors. Philosophies for Sale*, trans. A. M. Harmon, Loeb Classical Library 54, Cambridge, MA: Harvard University Press, 2015.

Lyotard, Jean François, *Enthusiasm: The Kantian Critique of History*, trans. Georges van den Abbeele, Palo Alto: Stanford University Press, 2009.

Lyotard, Jean François, *Lessons on the Analytic of the Sublime*, trans. Elizabeth Rotenberg, Palo Alto: Stanford University Press, 1994.

Sartre, Jean-Paul, *The Transcendence of the Ego*, New York: Hill & Wang, 1991.

Schrift, Alan, *Twentieth-Century French Philosophy: Key Themes and Thinkers*, London: Blackwell Publishing, 2006.

Simondon, Gilbert, 'The Genesis of the Individual', in *Incorporations (Zone: 6)*, ed. Jonathan Crary, New York: Zone Books, 1992, pp. 297–319.

Simondon, Gilbert, *L'Individuation psychique et collective*, Paris: Aubier, 1989.

Whitehead, A. N., *Process and Reality*, New York: Free Press, 1969.

Wittgenstein, Ludwig, *Culture and Value*, trans. Peter Finch, Chicago: University of Chicago Press, 1984.

Wittgenstein, Ludwig, *Tractatus Logico-Philosophicus* [1921; English edn 1922], trans. Bertrand Russell, 2nd edn, London: Routledge, 2001.

Index

9 781474 482943